DAT

MAY 0 9 '92
MAY 1 1 '92
JUL 2 8 '92
NOV 1 5 '92

WITHDRAWN
WRIGHT STATE UNIVERSITY LIBRARIES

COLS WRIGHT STATE UNIVERSITY
UNIVERSITY LIBRARY

0 00 13 0237223 8

14.95
80P

THE RESEARCH BOOK FOR GIFTED PROGRAMS

by

NANCY POLETTE

Book Design by Jodi Barklage

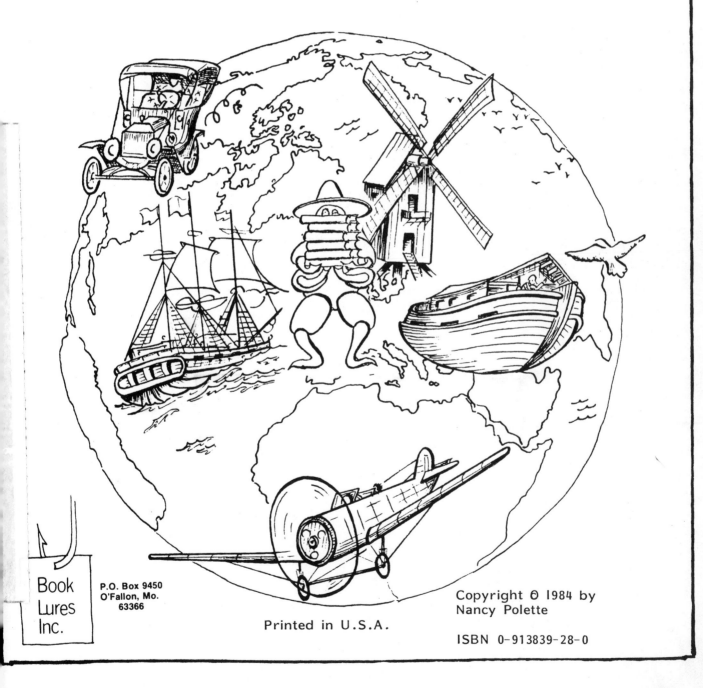

Book
Lures
Inc.

P.O. Box 9450
O'Fallon, Mo.
63366

Printed in U.S.A.

Copyright © 1984 by
Nancy Polette

ISBN 0-913839-28-0

ACKNOWLEDGEMENTS

The author is indebted to the following persons and agencies for their contributions to this work.

LC
3993.2
.P6
1984

Contributing Authors

Joyce Juntune, Executive Director National Association for Gifted Children. Thinking Skills from Project Reach.

Virginia Mealy, Resource Teacher, Riverview Gardens School District St. Louis County, MO. R.I.S.E. The Research Process

Flora Wyatt, Asst. Professor, Dept. of Curriculum and Instruction University of Kansas. Research Cards for Primary and Middle Grades

Agencies

Davenport, Iowa Public Schools. Darrell Lietz, Dir. Basic Instructional Services. Tag-A-Talent Board and Questions

Missouri Dept. of Elementary and Secondary Education. Richard L. King, Coor. Curriculum Unit. Critical Reading Skills

Missouri Dept. of Elementary and Secondary Education, Bob Roach, Dir. Gifted Programs. Newspaper Book Report and Local History Unit.

Missouri Dept. of Conservation. Larry Behrens, Ed. Consultant. Cemetery Unit

Northern Assoc. California School Librarians. Esther Franklin, Cons. Research Skills Taxonomy

Reproduction Rights

The purchaser is granted reproduction rights of 30 copies of any student activity pages in this book FOR EDUCATIONAL USE ONLY during any one school year.

THE RESEARCH BOOK FOR GIFTED PROGRAMS

by

Nancy   Polette

CONTENTS

INTRODUCTION
Relating Characteristics of the Gifted to Instruction 1
Model for Research and Independent Study Activities 4

SECTION ONE: THINKING SKILLS   5
Introducing Thinking Skills: Fluency............................. 6
Mind Stretchers 7
Flexibility, Originality, Elaboration 8
Critical Thinking 9
Decision Making 10
Creative Problem Solving 11
Critical Reading 14
Forming Concepts 15
Judging Sources 16
Defending 17
Analyzing 18
Working from a Hypothesis 19
Communication Skills 20
Identifying Levels of Thinking 22
Tag-A-Talent Board 23
Tag-A-Talent Quiz One 24
Tag-A-Talent Quiz Two 25

SECTION TWO: RESEARCH SKILLS FOR GIFTED STUDENTS   26
A Taxonomy of Research Skills 28
Dictionary Skills: Frog and Toad 34
Dictionary Skills: Incognito Titles 35
Encyclopedia Skills: Track Down 36
Encyclopedia Skills: Reference Math 37
Tic Tac Toe with Animal Facts 38
Mei Lei 39
Card Catalog: Scary Books 40
Card Catalog: Best of Science Fiction 41
Dewey Decimal System: Baffling Battles 42
Dewey Decimal System: Mythology Mystery 43
Using Reference Sources 44
Atlas Practice 45
Useful Quick Reference Handbooks 47
Life of A Truck Driver(Reference Book Practice) 48
Almanac Practice 49
Researching the Fifty States 50
Reference Source Quick Check 51

SECTION THREE: RESEARCH ACTIVITIES FOR PRIMARY GRADES   52
   Observational Research Cards 53
   Calendars 53
   Hair 53
   Homes 54
   Desserts 54
   Soda Straws 55
   Balls 55
   Potatoes 56
   Shoes 56
   Learning About Apples 57
   Looking Around Our School 58
   Windows and Doors 59
   ABCs of Non Fiction Research: 26 Activities 60
   Picture Research: Ocean Life 67
   Picture Research: Insects 68
   Picture Research: Birds 69
   Picture Research: Community Helpers 70
   Book Research Cards 71
      Dinosaurs, Mammoths, Microbes 71
      Oxygen, Planets, Bigfoot 72
      Salt, Rot, Dinosaurs 73
      Lizards, Animal Weapons, Caves 74
      Icebergs, Mars, Scientists 75
      Cocoa, Zoo Babies, Creatures with Pockets 76
      Volcanoes, Whales, Oceans 77
      UFOs, Park Rangers. Indians 78
      Forests, Robots, Loch Ness 79
      Seahorse, Eskimo, Jungles 80
      Snails, Microscopes, Moon 81
      Alligator, Octopus, Brain 82
      Glaciers, Australia, Pollution 83
      Signals, Universe, Spiders 84
      Sea, Teeth, Prove It! 85
   My Research Project 86

SECTION FOUR: RESEARCH AND THE MIDDLE GRADES   87
   The Research Process 88
   A Story to Share 89
   Stating the Problem 91
   Listing Known Information 92
   Listing Questions 93
   Listing Sources 94
   Locating Sources 95
   Acquiring Information 96
   Taking Notes 97
   Outlining 98
   Preparing the Finished Product 99
   Product Ideas 100
   Notetaking Form 101
   Bibliography Form 102
   Outline Form 103
   Interviewing Form 104
   Research Summary Sheet 105
   Research Evaluation 106

Research Cards Based on Specific Books 107
Automobiles, Famous Explorers 107
Inventors, American Revolution 108
Money, Horses 109
Colonial America, Stonehenge 110
Plants, Web of Nature 111
Earth, Fifty States 112
Animal Olympics, Sharks 113
Culture Comparison Chart 114
Mini-Newspaper 115
Animals in the News 118
Newspaper and Productive Thinking 119
Learning About Gifted Persons: Catnip Bill 122
A Study of Biography Using Bloom's Taxonomy 124
Images of Greatness 125
Biography: Inventors 126
The Annual Arts Award 127
Photo Puzzlers: One 128
Photo Puzzlers: Two 129

SECTION FIVE: RESEARCH ACTIVITIES GRADES SIX THROUGH EIGHT 130
Making the Goal in Research 131
Process and Product 132
Asking Good Questions 133
Research Cards: Upper Grades 134
Alcoholism 134
Biography 134
Capital Punishment 135
ERA 135
Folk Literature 136
Future Studies :One 136
Future Studies: Two 137
Great Goofs! 137
Leadership 138
Lyrics (Rock) 138
Stock Market 139
Television Shows 139
Comparison Research 140
Taking A Poll 141
Learning Styles 142
Leadership Study 144
Moral Development 145
Crossroads: Decisions Made by Gifted Persons 146
Researching Great Decisions in History 148
Power: Use and Abuse 149
Field Investigation: The Cemetery 151
Producing a Local History Reference Book 155
Evaluation 168

ANSWER KEYS   169

INTRODUCTION

Independent learning does not just happen. It requires motivation and task commitment, facility with research skills and sources, flexible thinking and problem-solving skills and a high degree of productive and critical thinking ability. A program in independent study for gifted students must take into consideration all of the above components but even more important, the gifted independent study program must consider the basic needs of gifted students.

Gifted students ARE different. Many are already independent learners who need purpose and direction. Most are fluent thinkers with many questions and ideas, willing to take risks, challenged by complexity, elaborative and original in thinking, inquisitive, intuitive and imaginative. In addition, gifted students generally grasp and retain knowledge easily and are able to transfer learning to other disciplines. Because of these and other traits, the gifted student needs a program which is differentiated to speak to specific needs.

Any effective program for the gifted must be tailored to individual student interests and to the development of wider interests through exposure to a wide variety of resources. Projects must be based on real-life situations whenever possible and should have as their focus the solving of relevant problems. When given the opportunity for problem-solving, students should have the follow-up experience of trying their solutions and facing the fact that their solutions may fail!

Skills are of necessity, an important part of the independent study program. However, the acquisition of research skills should be approached in a functional manner...specific skills taught as the need for the skill arises...rather than as a series of unrelated exercises. The SKILLS TAXONOMY included in this book can serve as a checklist for individual students to make sure all essential skills have been acquired before the student begins a project requiring those skills.

CHARACTERISTICS OF GIFTED STUDENTS

ABILITY TO PLAN, ORGANIZE, EXECUTE, JUDGE.

QUESTIONING

NDEPENDENT LEARNER

RETAINS KNOWLEDGE TRANSFERS LEARNING

CHARACTERISTICS
OF
GIFTED
STUDENTS

Activities in THE RESEARCH BOOK FOR GIFTED PROGRAMS have been carefully designed and field tested with gifted students to speak to the needs of the gifted learner. Critical and productive thinking activities are presented first as all research projects depend on facility with higher level thinking processes.

Skills of location, acquisition, organization, recording, communication and evaluation are presented in a manner designed to appeal to the inquisitive and curious nature of the gifted child. Divergent approaches are stressed in both the acquisition and utilization of skills.

In addition to building skills activities and projects based on the specific needs of the gifted, consideration has also been given to the developmental stages of these students. Activities included for primary children stress hands-on observational experiences. Initial research projects which do require printed materials are designed to help the child strengthen his or her skills of observation. It should be noted that the many higher level thinking activities included in this text are as appropriate for young children as for older learners.

Moving students from teacher-directed to self-directed learning is no easy task. The goal is for the student to select his or her content, determine the time frame of the study, and select the questions, resources, activities, product and evaluative procedure for the study. Obviously, moving students toward independent learning is a gradual process. THE RESEARCH BOOK FOR GIFTED PROGRAMS is intended as an aid to assist in each step of this process.

ELABORATIVE, ORIGINAL

INQUISITIVE, INTUITIVE
IMAGINATIVE: SEES
UNUSUAL RELATIONSHIPS

CHALLENGED BY COMPLEXITY

THINKS IN ABSTRACT TERMS

RISK TAKER

HAS MANY IDEAS

RESEARCH AND THE GIFTED STUDENT

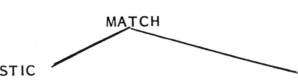

MATCH

CHARACTERISTIC   STRATEGY

FLUENT/FLEXIBLE THINKER   STUDENT-DEVELOPED QUESTIONS
                                       WIDE VARIETY OF SOURCES
                                       TRANSFER OF KNOWLEDGE

ORIGINAL THINKER   EXAMINE MANY POINTS OF VIEW
                                       USE OF DISCREPANCIES
   ANALOGIES & FORCED ASSOCIATION
                                       ENCOURAGE ORIGINAL PRODUCTS

OBSERVANT
INQUISITIVE   INDUCTIVE LEARNING!
CURIOUS   HIGHER LEVEL QUESTIONS
                                       WORK FROM A HYPOTHESIS

RISK TAKER   COMPLEX PROBLEMS
LIKES COMPLEXITY
                                       LEARN ABOUT CREATIVE PEOPLE
                                       AND PROCESSES

RESPONSIBLE/INDEPENDENT   SELF-DIRECTED LEARNING
LEARNER   ACCELERATED SKILLS ACQUISITION
GRASPS & RETAINS KNOWLEDGE   VERTICAL ACCELERATION OF
EASILY   KNOWLEDGE BASE

INTUITIVE/IMAGINATIVE   RANDOM SEARCH TECHNIQUES
                                       DEVELOP FORECASTING ABILITY
                                       UNIQUE APPLICATION OF
                                            COMMUNICATION SKILLS

3

THE GIFTED LEARNER

MODEL FOR RESEARCH AND INDEPENDENT STUDY ACTIVITIES

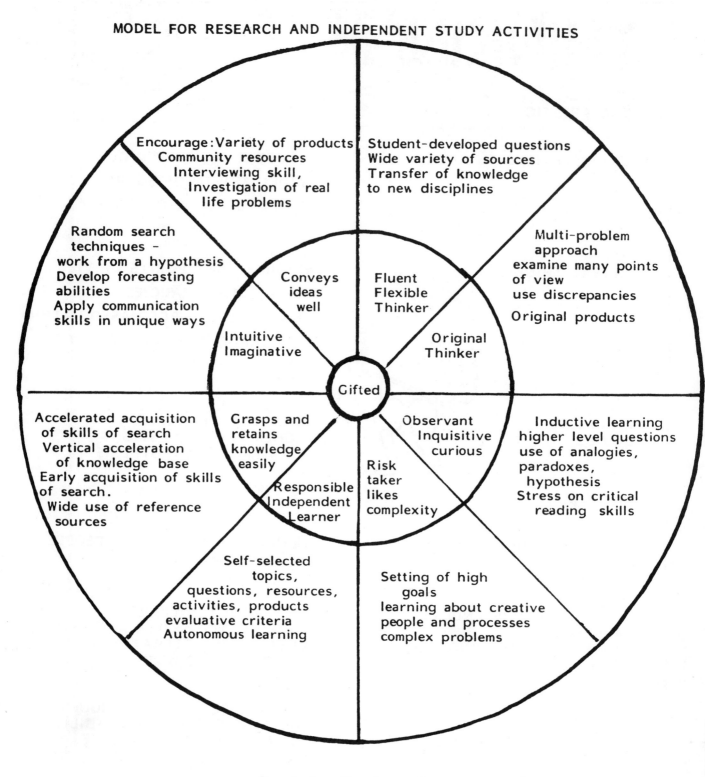

Encourage: Variety of products
Community resources
Interviewing skill,
Investigation of real
life problems

Student-developed questions
Wide variety of sources
Transfer of knowledge
to new disciplines

Random search
techniques -
work from a hypothesis
Develop forecasting
abilities
Apply communication
skills in unique ways

Multi-problem
approach
examine many points
of view
use discrepancies

Original products

Conveys
ideas
well

Fluent
Flexible
Thinker

Intuitive
Imaginative

Original
Thinker

Gifted

Accelerated acquisition
of skills of search
Vertical acceleration
of knowledge base
Early acquisition of skills
of search.
Wide use of reference
sources

Grasps and
retains
knowledge
easily

Observant
Inquisitive
curious

Inductive learning
higher level questions
use of analogies,
paradoxes,
hypothesis
Stress on critical
reading skills

Risk
taker
likes
complexity

Responsible
Independent
Learner

Self-selected
topics,
questions, resources,
activities, products
evaluative criteria
Autonomous learning

Setting of high
goals
learning about creative
people and processes
complex problems

Curriculum Development
for
Gifted Programs

Research model developed by Nancy Polette.   ℗ 1984

4

THINKING SKILLS

Characteristic

Gifted students are independent thinkers. They tend to form opinions without consulting established authorities. It is easier to know all the answers than to think of the right questions to ask!

Curriculum Implications

Introduction of productive and critical thinking skills, critical reading skills and effective communication skills.

SKILLS INCLUDED IN THIS SECTION

ARE:

Productive Thinking
- Fluency
- Flexibility
- Originality
- Elaboration

Critical Thinking
- Planning
- Forecasting
- Decision Making
- Problem Solving
- Evaluation

Critical Reading
- Associating Ideas
- Context Clues
- Classifying
- Concept Development
- Analysis of Data,
  fallacies, judgements
  points of view
  sources of information
- Extrapolating
- Inferring
- Hypothesizing

Communication Skills

Description within categories
Description of feelings
Comparisons and Relationships

Empathy
Non-verbal
Composition

THINKING SKILLS
Definitions and Warm-up Activities
(adapted from Project Reach with permission of Joyce Juntune)

FLUENCY

A. <u>Productive Thinking</u> is thinking of as many solutions as possible to a given problem. The kinds of productive thinking are:

1. <u>Fluency</u> is the ability to produce usually common responses to a given situation. The emphasis is on quantity rather than quality.

    a. The first responses are usually common responses.
    b. During a session of brainstorming, the best ideas come in the last 25% of the ideas given.
    c. Teachers should try to keep the flow going by:
        (1) looking for different ideas
        (2) encouraging "hitchhiking" (getting an idea from someone else)
        (3) deferring judgment - this is especially difficult for teachers, but the flow will not continue if the student waits to see if the idea is liked.
    d. Hypnotism has shown that there are many, many more ideas waiting in the subconscious.
    e. An accepting atmosphere must be provided.
    f. Writing answers can limit children's ability.
    g. One way of achieving fluency is to have the children work in pairs, having first one child talk on a particular subject and then switch to the other child and let him/her continue on the same subject.
    h. Sample warm-ups
        (1) "List as many geographic terms as you can." (Social Studies)
        (2) "List all the things you can think of that are found in the ocean." (Science)
        (3) "Write problems that have an answer of 24." (Math)
        (4) "List as many three-syllable words as you can." (Language Arts)

MIND STRETCHERS

Exercises to warm up thinking processes! How many answers can you give to each of the mind stretchers below:

NAME AS MANY ITEMS AS YOU CAN THAT ARE:

1. as important as the written word

2. as impossible to open as a can without a can opener

3. as useless as eyeglasses without lenses

4. as complex as the human mind

5. as intricate as a spider web

6. as wise as it is dangerous to perform

7. as often found together as a lock and a key

8. as obese as a whale

9. as unusual as a mother with ten sets of twins

10. as insignificant as a grain of sand

11. as frequently used as an Easter basket

12. as much a pair as shoes and socks

13. as strong as they are light in weight

14. as many sided as a pentagon

15. as bright as a spotlight

16. as infinite in variety as they are singular in use

17. as long as the Mississippi River

18. as deep as it is wide

19. as striped as a zebra

20. as funny as a clown car with ten clowns

21. as spotted as a kid with chickenpox

22. as utilitarian as they are decorative

23. as easy to build as they are to destroy

24. as happy as a winner at the end of a race

FLEXIBILITY

2. Flexibility is the ability to respond in a variety of categories. Flexibility is important because thinking can get stuck on one subject.

    a. Sample warm-ups
        (1) "Categorize 50 items related to U.S.Government. How many categories do you have?" (Social Studies)
        (2) "Look at your list of three-syllable words. How many of you listed foods? animals? furniture? What other categories could we use? How many categories did you have?" (Language Arts)
        (3) "List and categorize as many famous scientists as you can." (Science)
        (4) "How many different ways can you show the number 6? (Math)

ORIGINALITY

ELABORATION

3. Originality is the ability to make clever, unique responses. There are two kinds of originality:

    a. Ideas original to society
    b. Ideas original to this group at this particular time and place.
        (1) a child should not sit forever on the ownership of an idea
        (2) once an idea is out it forces the child to think of another
    c. Sample warm-ups
        (1) "Write a new ending for Cinderella." (Language Arts)
        (2) "Write original lyrics to a favorite song." (Music)
        (3) "Give an example of one way you would improve a chemical." (Science)
        (4) "What new idea could our class use to make money?" (Social Studies)

4. Elaboration is expanding a basic idea to make it more interesting and complete.

   a. It is taking what you want to get done and making it clear enough so that it can get done.
   b. Sample warm-ups
      (1) "Choose a three-syllable word from your list. How could you elaborate on that word?" (Story? Sentence? Picture? Song?) (Language Arts)
      (2) Hold up a dictionary. "How could we elaborate on this cover to make it more interesting and attractive?" (Language Arts)
      (3) Draw a circle on the board. "Who will come to the board and elaborate on this shape to change its appearance?" (Art, Math)
      (4) Add details to your description of the moon to clarify it. (Science)

CRITICAL THINKING

5. Planning is organizing a method for achieving a specific solution or outcome. The Planning process includes the following steps:

   a. Identification - the student states what he/she wants to do (problem or project) with enough additional information to explain what he/she plans to accomplish. Decision making precedes this step.
   b. Materials - the student lists the materials necessary to carry out the project.
   c. Steps - the child looks at all the steps involved in actually carrying out his/her plan. Organization of materials, time, and resources must be provided for.
   d. Problems - the student to consider problems he/she might encounter.
   e. Sample warm-ups
      (1) Plan a math game using triangles. (Math)
      (2) Plan a Thanksgiving feast for your classroom. (Social Studies)
      (3) Plan a demonstration of the principle of the pulley. (Science)

6. Forecasting is the ability to predict many different causes and/or effects of a given situation. Forecasting includes the following steps:

a. The student considers all the possible causes and results for a given situation. The student should think in terms of cause and effect.
The cause does not have to be related to the effect.
(1) One area (cause or effect) may be worked on at one time. Tell children you are only using part of the process.
(2) The guideline to be used in forecasting is flexibility. When you begin to think along category lines, you are able to get your mind out of a rut.
b. The student examines the quality of each prediction.
c. The student chooses his/her best cause and/or best effect.
d. The student gives reasons for his/her choice.
The ability to follow this process in forecasting carries over in determining behavior.
e. Sample warm-ups
(1) Suppose the government decreed that an entirely new system of measurement must be used throughout the country. What effects would this have? (Math)
(2) Suppose man could find a way to provide low cost energy that did not require the use of oil. What effects would this have? (Science/Social Studies)
(3) Forecast the causes and effects of not being able to use the telephone for one month. (Language Arts)

7. <u>Decision Making</u> follows the following steps:

a. Alternatives - the teacher encourages the student to think of many alternatives to a problem he/she wished to solve.
b. Criteria - the teacher assists the student in establishing criteria for weighing each alternative.
c. Weighing - the teacher assists the student in weighing his/her alternatives in terms of his/her criteria. The following grid may be used for this purpose.

Rating Low 1----5 High	Criteria	Criteria	Criteria
Alternative			
Alternative			
Alternative			
Alternative			

d. Sample warm-ups
1. "If you could only eat one kind of food for a whole week, what would you eat? Think of at least five alternatives. (choices) While you're thinking about your decisions, consider these criteria: (Social Studies)
(1) Do I like it?
(2) Will it be good for me?
(3) Can I afford it?
(4) Will my parents let me?
(5) Will I get tired of it?
Carefully make your choice. Give reasons for your choice."

2. "We have read many interesting stories. Which one do you think is the best? Think of three stories that you like. (These are your alternatives.) Consider the following criteria as you make your choice: (Language Arts)
    (1) Does it have a good ending?
    (2) Did it keep me interested?
    (3) Would I recommend it to a friend?
    Give three reasons for your choice."

8. Evaluation is the ability to weigh ideas, looking at the desirability and undesirability of each.

    a. It is an attempt to equalize both sides of an idea
    b. The following form may be used.

EVALUATION

Subject

Likes	Dislikes

    c. Sample warm-ups
    (When introducing evaluation, to avoid prejudice, push students to strive for the same number of positive and negative points.)
    1. Evaluate an editorial in your local paper. With what points do you agree? Disagree?
    2. "Evaluate the performance of the class yesterday. What is desirable about it? What is undesirable about it?" (Social Studies)
    3. Evaluate a book or a character from a story the class has read. "What did you find that was good about the story (or character)? What was bad about the book?" (Language Arts)

9. Creative Problem Solving is a process developed by Dr. Alex Osborne and Dr. Sidney Parnes that enables individuals to develop their creative skill and use it to help them solve problems. The CPS technique encourages the development of an open mind, generates the ability to produce quality and original ideas, and greater expression of curiosity.
    To insure a clear understanding of the steps of the CPS process at an elementary school age, it is wise to work on the concept of each step independently and then put all the steps together for the total process.
    There are some important factors that are prerequisite to work on any part of the process. When one is working in the beginning stages, it is important that the situation or activity be one that the students are not emotionally entangled with. The purpose is an understanding of the process, not proof of it.
    The basic rules for brainstorming or production of ideas underlie: every activity at every step:
    1. Produce many ideas.
    2. Hitchhike on other people's ideas
    3. Far-out ideas
    4. Defer judgment

WORKSHEET

Objective:

1. Fact Finding. Determine available facts stated in the problem. Use key words such as WHO, WHAT, WHEN, WHERE and WHY.

    _____

    _____

    _____

    _____

    What other information might you need? Be fluent and flexible in utilizing resources.

    _____

    _____

    _____

2. Problem Finding. Restate the problem at least three ways. Decide which statement most accurately defines the problem.

    1) _____

        _____

        _____

    2) _____

        _____

    3) _____

        _____

3. Idea Finding (Brainstorming, alternatives, etc.). Using the best problem statement, list as many possible solutions as you can think of. Sketch some pictures. Defer judgment. Don't evaluate, censor or judge. Anything goes! After you have made your list, circle the best ones.

_____

_____

_____

_____

_____

4. Solution Finding. What standards do you want the solution to meet when you have finished? List four or five criteria. Complete work towards solution.

_____

_____

_____

_____

_____

If several answers are possible, make a grid listing your best ideas down the side and your alternatives across the top (see a Solution Finding Matrix). Rate the ideas from one to five for each criteria. Work down, not across. Add the total. The highest number will have the best chance for success, according to your criteria.

5. Acceptance Finding. If there is only one possible correct solution, check the solution with the teacher. If several solutions were possible, list reasons why you selected yours.

_____

_____

_____

What steps would you use to implement your solutions?

_____

_____

_____

_____

CRITICAL

READING

B. CRITICAL READING SKILLS

1. Associating Ideas: Students can develop hypotheses about why they and others act as they do by using the following theoretical model developed by the Lakewood, Ohio project.

   MOTIVATING FORCES + RESOURCES + IMMEDIATE PHYSICAL

   SETTING = BEHAVIOR (Read + as interacts with)

   a. Motivating factors: the needs and feelings people try to satisfy
   b. Resources: an individual's abilities, skills, knowledge, perceptions and problem-solving methods
   c. Immediate physical setting: the surroundings in which the behavior occurs.

   Warm up activity: Why do you think Thomas Edison failed the third grade twice?
   Why were the ideas of Lister rejected by the medical community?

2. Using Context Clues: Combining reading skills and a knowledge base to increase comprehension.

   a. CLOZE PROCEDURE

   Deleting every fifth, seventh or tenth word in a passage beginning with the second sentence.

   (1) Example: INFLATION

   if everyone agrees that inflation is a grave problem, why is it so difficult to stop? One reason is that _____ people like to rail _____ rising prices, many also _____ some handsome benefits from _____. They have in effect _____ a constituency for inflation. Suppose you told _____ businessmen that you could _____ a magic wand and _____ the inflation rate to _____. They would think about _____ for a minute and _____ no. They have made _____ fixed commitments in loans _____ inventories that they would _____ want to live with.

14

3. Classification: Grouping terms for clearer understanding of a topic.

   a. Warm up activities

   (1) Name and group the world's dissenters.
   (2) Name and group chemicals essential to our lives.
   (3) Name and group types of governments.
   (4) Name and group the foods served in our school lunches.

FORMING CONCEPTS

4. Concept Development: Bringing together specific elements of a concept to form a rule.

LABEL	British Citizen
Positive examples:	Queen Elizabeth, Margaret Thatcher
Negative examples:	Abraham Lincoln, Michael Jackson

   ATTRIBUTES

   Essential — person
   born of British parents
   achieved British citizenship thru courts

   Nonessential — sex, age, race, intelligence

   RULE: A British citizen is one born of British parents, or made a citizen according to British law.

   ### TRY THIS!

   LABEL   Rock Star

   Positive Examples:

   Negative Examples:

   ATTRIBUTES

   Essential:

   Nonessential:

   RULE: A ROCK STAR IS _____

   _____

JUDGING

SOURCES

5. Judging Sources of Information: Determining reliability of what is read or heard or seen.

   a. Judging reports:
     (1) What are the time and space relationships between reporter and event?
     (2) Was the report first hand or second hand?
     (3) If not an eyewitness does the reporter tell who his source was? Is the source reliable?
     (4) What biases does the reporter have? (Background, affiliations, choice of words?)
     (5) Does the report agree with other independent reports?
     (6) Examine news stories in different papers about the same events using the criteria above. On what points do the stories agree? Disagree?
     (7) Judge information using a credibility continuum.

1	2	3	4	5
Totally Unreliable				Excellent Source

1	2	3	4	5
Biased				Objective

1	2	3	4	5
Uninformed in subject				Expert in subject

1	2	3	4	5
Dependent on hearsay				Eyewitness Observer

DEFENDING

6. Defending Judgments: The ability to support personal judgment with factual data.

    a. Warm Up Activity: Below are five headlines from U. S. newspapers. Rate these as to their impact on you as an individual and their impact on the nation. Supply data to support your judgment.

	Little impact			Much Impact	
(1) OPEC Nations Raise Oil Prices 10%					
Impact on me	1	2	3	4	5
Impact on U.S.	1	2	3	4	5
(2) Flu Epidemic Strikes Tokyo					
Impact on me	1	2	3	4	5
Impact on U.S.	1	2	3	4	5
(3) Russian Wheat Harvest Below Expectations					
Impact on me	1	2	3	4	5
Impact on U.S.	1	2	3	4	5
(4) Japan Agrees to Accept More Imports					
Impact on me	1	2	3	4	5
Impact on U.S.	1	2	3	4	5
(5) War in Mideast Accelerates					
Impact on me	1	2	3	4	5
Impact on U.S.	1	2	3	4	5

7. Analyzing Data: To make important discriminations concerning statements, readings and discussions according to various categories.

    a. Analysis of statements thru categorizing: Is the statement fact, opinion or definition?
    b. Analysis of issues: Have students categorize issues according to:
        (1) Fact/explanation issues (what happened, what is happening)
        (2) Definitional issues (What does it mean?)
        (3) Moral/value issues (Dealing with good or bad, right or wrong)
    c. Categorize the following issues:
        (1) Should all citizens be compelled by law to wear seatbelts?
        (2) The wearing of seatbelts should be required only of those riding in automobiles.
        (3) The forcing of the individual to wear a seatbelt is an infringement on personal liberty.

ANALYZING

8. Understanding Analogies: To clarify meanings of terms or relationships. Analogies are events related to each other based on a commonality.

    a. Warm up activities

        (1) Henry Hudson was to the Atlantic as Balboa was to the _____.
        (2) St. Louis is to Missouri as Toronto is to _____.
        (3) Gasoline is to automobile as _____ is to _____.
        (4) Sock is to shoe as _____ is to _____.
        (5) Atom is to energy as _____ is to _____.

9. Analyzing Fallacies in Reasoning: Assessing the logic of what is read.

    a. Types of fallacies

        (1) Confusing time and cause relationships: (Ex.: Since the Democrats were in power during World Wars I and II, therefore the Democrats caused the wars.)
        (2) False Analogies: (Ex.: Since this person was born in our town he/she will make a better mayor than someone who was born elsewhere.)
        (3) Stereotypic Ideas: Oversimplification of characteristics of groups or individuals. (Ex.: All librarians wear glasses. All women are poor drivers. All men are aggressive.)
        (4) Invalid Deductive Reasoning: Deductive reasoning refers to a major premise, a minor premise and a conclusion. (Ex.: All living things die. People are living things. Therefore all people will die.)

            Example of poor reasoning: Rattlesnakes are found in the desert.
            Charlie found a rattlesnake.
            Therefore Charlie must be in the desert.
        (5) Have students bring advertisements to class and analyze any fallacies found.

10. Extrapolating from Current Trends: Considering the implications of statistical trends for the future.

    a. Have students follow data for a period of time. (Food prices, stock market data, production data, population trends etc.) Analyze trends and predict effects for the future.
    b. Consider inventions of the past and their effect on society. Watch for news of new inventions and predict their effect on society.

WORKING FROM A HYPOTHESIS

11. Hypothesizing: Developing a question, statement, or generalization that could be tested.

   a. Study and interpret data source.
   b. Develop hypothesis: question or statement that shows a relationship between two or more items....If/then.
   c. State reasoning for hypothesis. List statements on which hypothesis is based.
   d. Determine a method for testing hypothesis. State conditions and procedures.
   e. Test hypothesis and record test results.
   f. Analyze results. Determine if hypothesis is valid or if additional information is needed.

   (1) Warm up activity

   Share (available as book or sound filmstrip from Random House) Jean George's THE WOUNDED BUTTERFLY. Read or show film to the point where the butterfly breaks its wing. State that at the end of the story the butterfly is able to migrate from the eastern U.S. to Mexico (a trip of 1500 miles). Ask students to hypothesize how this was possible. (Hypothesis can be tested by securing data on the life cycle and habits of the Monarch butterfly).

   Question: How could a butterfly who has broken a wing travel 1500 miles from the eastern U.S. to Mexico?

   When students have stated and tested a hypothesis finish sharing the story or film.

COMMUNICATION

SKILLS

C.   Communication Skills

<u>Communication</u> is the ability to express thought and ideas to others
and includes the following areas:

1. Description within categories - the teacher encourages the student
   to list many words within given categories.
   a. set categories
   b. list words
   c. put words together to write phrases, sentences, stories,
       poetry, etc.

2. Description of feelings - the teacher encourages the student to
   use a variety of words to describe his/her feelings and values.
   a. use empathy situations as they arise in classroom rather than
       trying to invent situations
   b. use pictures of moods and emotions

3. Comparisons and relationships - the teacher leads the students
   to make comparisons among things or show relationships and
   associations.
   a. it's good for the student to bring two things together for
       comparison
   b. he/she asks how they are alike and how they are different
   c. then he/she determines how they might be put together

4. Empathy - the teacher builds upon opportunities for students
   to share personal experiences or thoughts that are similar to the
   experiences or thoughts of others.
   a. this is a spontaneous situation
   b. it is verbally recognized when observed in students
   c. it cannot be pre-planned

5. Non-verbal - the teacher guides the student to become more
   skillful in interpreting and using non-verbal forms of communication
   to express his/her feelings, thoughts, and needs to others. These
   are progressive stages:
   a. throw out words and ask children to react with whole body
   b. give situations and ask children to react
   c. list occupations or categories and ask children to strike pose
       of one and then freeze
   d. in small groups create a circumstance and tell children to play
       a scene without discussing it with anyone - just look around
       and find a way to fit in
   e. portray an idea using a symbol

6. Composition - the teacher creates opportunities for the student to organize words into meaningful networks of meanings, thoughts, and needs

   questioning - asks questions about detail, but stays centered on subject

Relate the incident shown in these three drawings in an interesting way by adding as many details as possible.

7. Sample warm-ups
   a. Description within given categories
      "One part of communication is using descriptive words. Let's look at this snowball. What words describe how it looks? What words describe how it feels?"
   b. Description of feelings
      "Describe how you feel when you've called all your friends - accurately describe your feelings."
   c. Comparison/Relationships
      Give each student a cotton ball. "What words can you use to finish this sentence? Cotton is as white as ..."
   d. Empathy
      Empathy does not lend itself to written activity. It is most effectively developed when it is postively reinforced as it occurs in the classroom.
   e. Composition
      "Yesterday the mailman came to my house with a huge, gigantic package addressed to me. Then what do you think happened?"

      "Suppose you came to class one day and found a substitute teacher with no directions to follow. Compose, in your own mind, what you would need to tell him/her. Be sure your ideas are expressed clearly and concisely." Have the students orally give the directions as they would give them to the substitute.
   f. Non-verbal
      "Show me, using your face, how you feel when you eat a foot-long hot dog. Add your hands and body to help show. Now pretend you have had 35 hot dogs! Show how you feel."

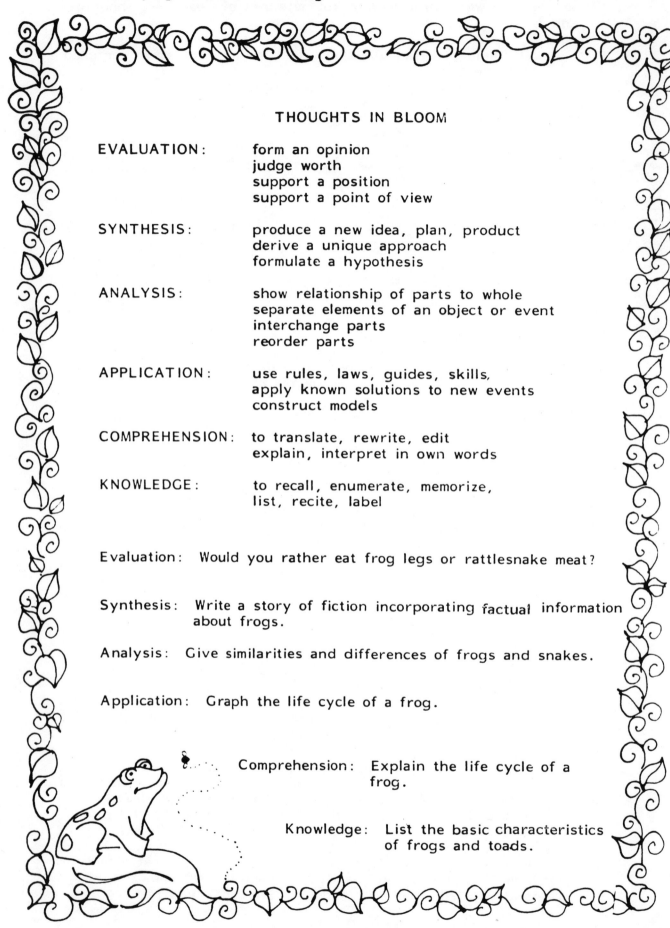

THOUGHTS IN BLOOM

EVALUATION: form an opinion
judge worth
support a position
support a point of view

SYNTHESIS: produce a new idea, plan, product
derive a unique approach
formulate a hypothesis

ANALYSIS: show relationship of parts to whole
separate elements of an object or event
interchange parts
reorder parts

APPLICATION: use rules, laws, guides, skills,
apply known solutions to new events
construct models

COMPREHENSION: to translate, rewrite, edit
explain, interpret in own words

KNOWLEDGE: to recall, enumerate, memorize,
list, recite, label

Evaluation: Would you rather eat frog legs or rattlesnake meat?

Synthesis: Write a story of fiction incorporating factual information about frogs.

Analysis: Give similarities and differences of frogs and snakes.

Application: Graph the life cycle of a frog.

Comprehension: Explain the life cycle of a frog.

Knowledge: List the basic characteristics of frogs and toads.

TAG A TALENT BOARD

PRODUCTIVE THINKING	FORECASTING	DECISION MAKING	PLANNING	COMMUNICATION
The Student expresses many ideas tho not all of the highest quality (Fluency)	The student predicts many different causes/effects of a given situation	The student gives many alternatives to a problem solution in terms of limitations, relevancy	Student identifies his project with enough details about the basic idea to explain what he wants to do	Student produces many words that fit different categories.
The student expresses a variety of kinds of responses (Flexibility)		The student is able to weigh alternatives in terms of his/her needs and goals	The student is sensitive to problems that could arise as he works on his project.	The student uses a variety of words to describe his feelings and his values.
The student expresses unusual uncommon responses, tho not all ideas prove to be of use. (Originality)		The student is able to make a final judgment in terms of alternatives.	The student is able to organize materials, time and resources necessary to carry out his project.	Student expresses words and ideas to make comparisons and to show relationships among things.
The student builds onto a basic idea by adding details to make it more interesting or complete (Elaboration)		The student is able to defend his/her decision giving as many reasons as he/she can for his/her choice		Student participates in others' feelings and ideas by sharing similar experiences or thoughts of his own.
				Student organizes words into meaningful networks of ideas yielding a product.
				Student can interpret and use non-verbal forms of communication.

Check your understanding of higher level thinking skills. Match each definition given above with the independent study activities listed on the next page.

Tag a Talent Board and Questions adapted from Davenport, Iowa Gifted Program Materials with permission.

CHECK YOUR THINKING SKILLS

for Independent Study

SET ONE

1. The student is using many words to describe a rock for a science display.

2. The student is brainstorming many ways to improve a toy.

3. Student draws the most unusual thing to be found at the end of the rainbow .

4. The student is stating causes for an earthquake and predicting effects of a 9.5 quake.

5. Student is using different words to tell how he feels on a cool fall day.

6. Student gives more information in expanding ideas on how to use a tin can.

7. Student records his final career choice.

8. Student states intention to design a mosaic.

9. Student thinks of different uses of a paper bag.

10. Student composes a poem about the joy of being an American citizen.

11. Students use a set of criteria to decide which Arrow book to buy.

12. Student shares problems he/she anticipates in setting up a science exhibit.

13. Student adds details to chalk drawing.

14. Student records many reasons why he/she chose history as a major.

15. Student compares yellow flowers to many other yellow things.

16. Student lists steps, materials and problems in building a birdhouse.

17. Student pantomines how a banana feels being peeled.

18. Student shares a surprising incident like one his friend has had.

DIRECTIONS: Write the number of each activity in the set above on the Tag-A-Talent board. Place the number in the square which best describes the thinking process involved.

(Answer Key Page 169)

CHECK YOUR THINKING SKILLS

for Independent Study

SET TWO

1. Students are brainstorming as many things as possible that operate on a base 2 system.

2. Student wrote many reasons why he wanted a Miami vacation.

3. Student makes many predictions as to the cause of a car accident.

4. Student uses many different words to describe a roller coaster ride.

5. Student tells the class about a science poster he is going to design.

6. Student gives more information to expand his idea on a new way to use aluminum foil.

7. Student lists a set of criteria to help in making a choice between two games.

8. Student is recording many different things mud is as squishy as.

9. Committee gives a list of all the possible colors the play backdrop can be painted.

10. Student is composing a get-well message to send to a hospitalized classmate.

11. Students are asked to wonder about the variety of ways messages are relayed.

12. Student records materials, resources, and steps to take to plant a garden.

13. After listening to many musical selections student chooses the one most pleasing.

14. Student uses body movements to express fun at the beach.

15. After studying Indian sign language the student is asked to invent a new word and a unique way to write a message.

16. Student expresses sympathy for a story character by relating to personal experience.

17. Student lists possible problems he may have in devising a math game.

18. Student uses many single words to describe a secret object in the room.

DIRECTIONS: Write the number of each activity in the set above on the Tag-A-Talent board. Place the number in the square which best describes the thinking process involved.

(Answer Key Page 169)

CURIOUS

RESEARCH SKILLS

ABILITY TO PLAN, ORGANIZE, EXECUTE JUDGE.

QUESTIONING

RISK TAKER

FOR
GIFTED STUDENTS

HAS MANY IDEAS

ACTIVE

Just as the writer must have a grasp of the basic tools of writing before using those tools in creative ways, the pursuer of knowledge must have competency in the skills of search in order to analyze, synthesize and evaluate information.

The taxonomy which follows gives both an entry level and a proficiency level for each skill listed. These levels indicate the grade at which the skill is usually introduced in most classrooms.

In differentiating skill development for the gifted student, acceleration or introduction of the skills at earlier levels is often suggested. In addition, the skills must be presented and used in both a challenging and functional manner to provide for the unique characteristics of these students.

E
X
A
M
P
L
E

SKILL: DICTIONARY USE

CHARACTERISTIC OF THE GIFTED: CHALLENGED BY COMPLEXITY

ACTIVITY: The following groups of synonyms represent titles of well-known books. Use the dictionary or thesaurus to find the meanings of the words. Give the book title.

1. PROCREATED UNINHIBITED (answer: Born Free)

2. INITIAL YIELD   (answer: First Crop)

3. GRIMALKIN IN GALOSHES (answer: Puss in Boots)

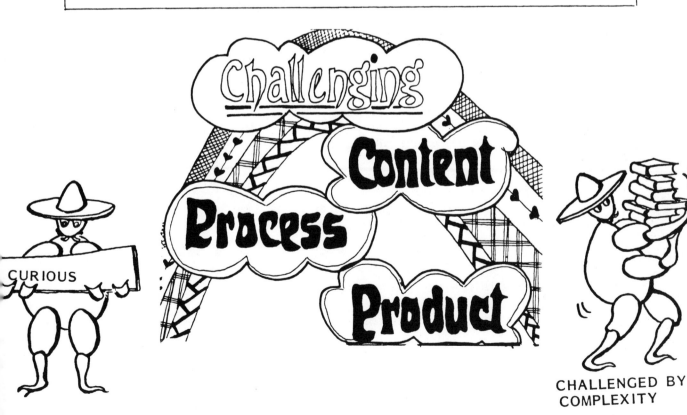

CURIOUS

Challenging Content Process Product

CHALLENGED BY COMPLEXITY

A TAXONOMY OF RESEARCH SKILLS

(developed by the Northern California School Librarians' Association. Used with permission)

Sample Behavioral Objectives: 1. Given the topic ARTS AND CRAFTS, 5th grade studen will be able to find the article "Fabric Painting With Mud," in <u>Ebony Jr.</u> within a ten-minute search. 2. After viewing sound film strip, 8th grade student can prepare note on 4 X 6 card which summarizes information found on whale migration.

SKILLS	PRI K-3	INT 4-6	JH 7-9	HS 10-12
I. Basic Skills				
A. Demonstrates competency in Topic Selection				
1. Verbalizes interest in topic generally	E-------	P	P	P
2. Can suggest area for research	E-------	P	P	P
3. Can limit scope of topic		E-------	-------	---P
4. Verbalizes need (personal or assigned) for research		E---P		P
5. Verbalizes intended use of information found and can suggest form of communicating findings		E------P		P
B. Understands general research procedures				
1. Verbalizes need for perfecting locational skills	E------P		P	P
2. Perceives value of making outline				
a. Makes an outline voluntarily		E---P		P
b. Seeks help on outlining techniques		E---P		P
c. Demonstrates proficiency in outlining		E---P		P
3. Demonstrates awareness of importance of notes				
a. Verbalizes intent to take notes		E---P		P
b. Converses about forms of note-taking		E---P		P
c. Begins note taking voluntarily		E------P		P
d. Seeks assistance in developing proficiency in note-taking		E---P		P
e. Demonstrates proficiency in note-taking				
1. Notes show standard bibliographic form		E------P		P
2. Notes demonstrate ability to abbreviate		E------P		P
3. If records kept in another form, can verbalize reasons specific to project		E------P		P
C. Demonstrates awareness of needed Reading skills				
1. Can verbalize difference between scanning and full comprehension reading		E----P		P
2. Can complete comprehension reading within a specific time		E----P		P

NOTE: E indicates entry level. P indicates proficiency level.

S K I L L S	PRI K-3	INT 4-6	JH 7-9	HS 10-12
D. Demonstrates awareness of Listening/Viewing skills				
1. Can demonstrate competency in retaining information by above techniques in short verbal interview	E------P		P	P
E. Understands importance of planning and preparation of communication about research				
1. Independently chooses written or recorded mode for reporting		E------P		P
2. If illustrations are to be used, selects with precision		E------P		P
3. Demonstrates familiarity with term "plagerism"		E------P		P
4. Cites sources quoted directly		E------P		P
F. Demonstrates understanding of Bibliography				
1. Can verbalize reasons for preparation of Bibliography		E--------P		
2. Uses notes accumulated in preparation of Bibliography		E--------P		
3. Seeks consistent form for entries		E--------P		
4. Follows form chosen		E--------P		
G. Understands possibilities to communicate in other modes than written report				
1. Verbalizes possibilities for recorded or photographic report	E----------P			
2. Seeks assistance in preparation of non-written report	E----------P			
3. Completes report in audio or photographic form		E----P		P
II. Locational Skills: Demonstrates Understanding and Facility Needed to Find Materials				
A. Can locate material on shelf through use of call number				
1. Understands ten basic classifications of Dewey decimal system	E----P		P	P
2. Understands parts of call numbers				
a. Classification number, including decimal arrangement and meaning	E----------P			
b. Author letters	E----------P			
c. Special symbols	E----------P			
3. Understands differences in call number and symbols used to designate non-fiction, fiction, easy books, biography, story collections, reference, etc.	E----------P			

SKILLS	PRI K-3	INT 4-6	JH 7-9	HS 10-12
4. Understands special symbols for audio-visual materials		E---	---P	P
5. Perceives relationships in classification systems				
a. Can distinguish between Dewey and L.O.C. call number				E---P
b. Recognizes minumum number of L.O.C. divisions necessary for special research				E---P
B. Can use catalogs effectively to find material desired and uses information on card or in book catalog to find material on shelf				
1. Identifies type of catalog (dictionary, divided)	E---	---P	P	P
2. Uses drawer labels and guide cards in search	E---	---P	P	P
3. Understands arrangement of cards (Alphabetical, chronological, subheadings, filing rules for abbreviations, numerals, type of entry, etc.)	E---	---P	P	P
4. Can distinguish between title and subject cards	E---	---P	P	P
5. Can distinguish between books by an author and about an author	E---	---P	P	P
C. Understands and interprets accurately information found on catalog cards and uses it as needed for further research				
1. Bibliographic information on card (author, title, imprint, collation, annotation, tracings)		E---	---P	P
2. Cross references (see and see also – types of reference cards)	E---	---P	P	P
III. Skills Needed in Using Reference Works				
A. Recognizes and interprets elements which distinguish reference works and provide insight into their purposes:				
1. Title page information	E---	---P	P	P
2. Copyright date	E---	---P	P	P
3. Prefatory material		E---	---P	P
4. Accuracy, authority		E---	---P	P
5. Contents and coverage	E---	---P	P	P
6. Intended reader		E---	---P	P
7. Amount and kind of information (Does it define, describe, identify, give overview, summarize, discuss fully, in depth, etc.?)		E---	---	---P
8. Arrangement/format (Alphabetically, categorically, by broad subjects, chronologically, etc.)	E---	---	---	---P

S K I L L S	PRI K-3	INT 4-6	JH 7-9	HS 10-12
9. Location and form of index (one or more, alphabetical, subjects, coverage, cross references, symbols used, etc.)		E----P	P	P
10. Special features (illustrations, maps, bibliographies, appendix, footnotes, keys, symbols, charts, diagrams, etc.)		E------	----P	P
B. Demonstrates facility in approach to use of reference books				
1. Alphabetizing	E------	P	P	P
2. Volume numbers and letters	E------	P	P	P
3. Key words	E------	P	P	P
4. Subject headings	E------	P	P	P
5. Cross references	E------	P	P	P
C. By use of locational evaluative skills, demonstrates facility in choosing reference work best suited to purpose	E------	------	------	--P
V. Demonstrates Understanding and Facility in Use of the Dictionary				
A. Recognizes kinds and demonstrates ability to choose appropriate dictionary				
1. Abridged and their features	E----	--P	P	P
2. Unabridged and their features		E---	------	--P
3. Special language dictionaries, including thesauri, and their uses		E---	------	--P
4. Audio dictionaries	E---	------	--P	P
B. Understands organization of material and demonstrates facility in finding needed information				
1. Alphabetical arrangement (to the 4th letter)	E------	P	P	P
2. Thumb index		E----P	P	P
3. Guide words (2 ways)		E---P	P	P
4. Definitions	E------	P	P	P
5. Multiple entries for same word		E----P	P	P
6. Explanatory pages		E---	------	--P
7. Guides to words you cannot spell		E----P	P	P
8. Special sections		E---	------	--P
9. Comparative features of abridged or unabridged		E---	------	--P
10. Pronunciation keys (including accent, etc.)	E------	--P	P	P
C. Recognizes and understands kinds of information given for each work entry in dictionary				
1. Meaning (alternative meanings)	E------	------	--P	P
2. Spelling (alternative spellings)	E------	------	--P	P
3. Pronunciation	E------	P	P	P
4. Syllabication		E---P	P	P

SKILLS	PRI K-3	INT 4-6	JH 7-9	HS 10-12
5. Grammar (parts of speech)		E------	---P	P
6. Prefixes, suffixes, roots		E---	--P	P
7. Synonyms, antonyms		E------	---P	P
8. Usage/Etymologies		E---		---P
9. Other information (chronological usage, etc.)		E-----		---P
V. Demonstrates Understanding and Use of The Encyclopedia				
A. Recognizes kinds of encyclopedias and their intended use				
1. Juvenile	E---		----P	P
2. Popular adult		E---	---P	P
3. Scholarly adult				E----P
4. One-volume		E---		---P
5. Special subjects	E---			---P
6. Encyclopedia yearbooks		E------	---P	P
7. Audio encyclopedia		E---	---P	P
B. Demonstrates ability to choose set appropriate to need and purpose				
1. Coverage	E---			---P
2. Intended reader	E---			---P
3. Timeliness			E----P	P
4. Authority		E---	----P	P
5. Ease in use, arrangement	E-		----P	P
6. Updated by yearbooks		E---	--P	P
C. Demonstrates facility in locating information by means of:				
1. Alphabetizing (word-by-word, or letter-by-letter)	E---	----P	P	P
2. Volume Numbers/Letters	E---	----P	P	P
3. Key words		E----	--P	P
4. Guide words		E---P	P	P
5. Cross references	E-	-----P	P	P
6. Indexes (organization, symbols, differences)		E---		---P
7. Illustrations/diagrams/charts	E-		------P	P
8. Bibliographies		E---		---P
9. Special keys/symbols		E---		---P
10. Compares entry in different sets		E---		---P
VI. Demonstrates Ability to Use Periodicals, Newspapers, and Related Indexes Effectively				
A. Recognizes different types and how to locate them				
1. Intended use and reader	E---			---P
2. Frequency of publication (daily, weekly, monthly, bi-monthly, etc.)		E-----	-P	P

Taxonomy developed by the Northern California School Librarians' Association under direction of Esther Franklin. Used with permission.

S K I L L S	PRI K-3	INT 4-6	JH 7-9	HS 10-12
3. Current and back issues		E———	———P	P
4. Where indexed		E———	———P	P
5. Differences between volumes and issues		E———	———P	P
B. Recognizes different types of applicable indexes and demonstrates facility in their use				
1. Subject Index to Children's Magazines	E———	———P	P	P
2. Abridged Reader's Guide		E———	———P	P
3. Reader's Guide			E———	———P
4. Other magazine indexes (National Geographic, etc.)	E———	———	———	———P
5. Newspaper indexes			E———	———P
6. Can interpret all symbols and keys	E———	———	———P	P
C. Chooses magazines and newspapers for various purposes				
1. General information		E———	———	———P
2. Research information		E———	———	———P
3. Pleasure, enjoyment (fiction, fact, illustrations)	E———	———P	P	P
4. Current subjects		E———	———P	P
5. Browsing	E———	———P	P	P
II. Other Reference Works: Recognizes Different Types of Reference Works Most Commonly Utilized, Demonstrates an Understanding of Their Special Purpose, and Shows Facility in Using				
A. Almanacs, yearbooks		E———	———P	P
B. Handbooks, directories			E———	———P
C. Bibliographic (general, special, reading/listening/viewing) lists	E———	———	———	———P
D. Collections, e.g., poetry, quotations, short story, biography, etc.		E———	———P	P
E. Atlases, gazetteers, globes		E———	———P	P
F. Indexes				
1. Fiction Index				E———P
2. Poetry and drama indexes (Granger, etc.)		E———	———	———P
3. Short Story Index		E———	———	———P
4. Education Index				E———P
5. Vertical File		E———	———	———P
6. Biography Index		E———	———	———P
7. Illustration Index		E———	———	———P
8. Other indexes		E———	———	———P

READ

FROG AND TOAD ARE FRIENDS

Harper & Row   Arnold Lobel
1970

Frog and Toad have five adventures in this book. When Toad oversleeps the early spring, Frog wakes him. When Frog is ill, Toad amuses him by trying to think of a story. Together they hunt a lost button, go swimming, and await a hoped-for letter.

Frogs and toads are amphibians. They spend part of their lives on land and part in the water. Frogs have smooth, damp skin while toads have dry, bumpy skin. Toads are fatter than frogs and can't jump as far. Both lay eggs in the water -- the toads in black strings and the frogs in bunches.

These words tell about frogs and toads:

gills	hibernate	croak
tail	eggs	jump
hop	lungs	bumpy
moist	dry	amphibian
string	tadpoles	cluster
climb	smooth	

1. Put a green circle around words that tell about frogs.

2. Put a brown circle around words that tell about toads.

3. Put an orange circle around words that tell about both.

4. Tell whether you would rather have a frog or a toad

   for a pet. _____

   Tell why_____

   _____

HINT: THE JUNIOR DICTIONARY WILL HELP YOU!

Buddies

Pals

DICTIONARY

INCOGNITO TITLES

Here are book titles which have been rewritten using synonyms. Use reference books such as dictionaries and thesauruses to identify them. They can be checked by using a card catalog or the media center's list of books in print.

A. 1. Procreated Unimpeded _____

2. The Beck of the Untamed Place _____

3. Inquisitive Mr. Washington Proceeds to the Infirmary _____

4. Rimy the Mortal Formed From White Crystal Precipitation _____

5. Chartreuse Ova In Addition to Smoked Razorback_____

6. The Wee Power Machine Which Possessed the Proficiency _____

7. Grimalkin in Galoshes _____

8. The Unrelenting Stannic Combatant _____

9. The Purloined Conflagration _____

10. The Repartee and Sagacity of Corpulent Mr. Einstein _____

B. Select five favorite book titles. Use a dictionary of synonyms or a thesaurus to develop incognito titles for others to solve.

1. _____

_____

2. _____

_____

3. _____

_____

4. _____

_____

5. _____

_____

DICTIONARY

ENCYCLOPEDIA SKILLS

Complete each blank using the encyclopedia.

Note that after the first item, there are two blanks in each. This is because the answer to the previous question becomes part of the next one.

TRACK DOWN the spy who hid microfilms of U. S. military secrets in a pumpkin on his farm in Maryland.

The horoscope is used by people who study (1) _____ .

In (1) _____ the part of the sky in which our solar system moves

is called the (2) _____ .

The tenth sign of the (2) _____ is (3) _____ or the

goat.

(3) _____ has the tail of a fish and the head of a (4)

_____ .

Two (4) _____s that grow (5) _____ are the angora and

the cashmere.

The softest and rarest (5) _____ comes from the vicuna of the (6)

_____ in Peru.

The only mountains higher than the (6) _____ are the (7)

_____ .

The name (7) _____ means "House of (8) _____ ."

(8) _____ crystals always have (9) _____ sides.

A (9) _____ shooter is a revolver with 5 or 6 (10)

_____ .

Solution: _____

On reaching number 10, students will find the answer in one of the entries with that title.

ENCYCLOPEDIA

REFERENCE MATH

Below are a series of reference activities which are then added, subtracted, mulitplied, or divided to reach the final answer. There are no fractions or remainders. All answers can be found in WORLD BOOK ENCYCLOPEDIA, though most are contained in other sources as well.

1. Begin with the age at which V. I. Lenin learned to read. _____

2. Multiply by the number of years Ulysses' journey lasted. _____

3. Multiply by the largest number of chambers a single-shot revolver has.

   _____

4. Divide by the number of John Aaron Lewis's stream music. _____

5. Divide by the number of words in Edison's first message on the

   phonograph. _____

6. Multiply by the number of the Constitutional Amendment that gave

   Washington, D.C. three votes in the electoral college. _____

7. Add the number of the acronym of Saul Alinsky's Woodlawn

   Organization. _____

8. Divide by the number James I became when he was made King of

   Scotland. _____

9. Add the number of the last pope named John. _____

10. Divide by the number of Brazil's last monarch. _____

Answer _____

USING THE PATTERN GIVEN ABOVE

DEVELOP YOUR OWN REFERENCE

MATH QUIZ FOR OTHERS TO SOLVE.

TIC-TAC-TOE WITH ANIMAL FACTS

Complete any three squares down, across, or diagonally. Use the books in the reference area to verify your answers. Identify your source in the square with the answer.

List one way a fish is adapted to living in water	Name an animal whose home is made of mud	Name an animal native to your state that no longer lives there
Name an insect you might find in an oak tree	Name a bird who was adversely affected by DDT	Name a mammal who who lives underground
Name an animal whose footprint you might find in your backyard	Name an animal whose actions directly affect you	List one way in which the shape of the bill influences what a bird eats

Source:

Source:

Source:

Source:

Source:

Source:

Source:

Source:

Source:

ENCYCLOPEDIA

Mei Li

Doubleday 1938   Thomas Handworth

It is the day before New Year's in China. Mei Li wants to go with her brother, San Yu, to the great city of Peking. However, only boys can go to the city. Mei Li sneaks away and bribes her brother to take her with him. She has many adventures. A generous child, she gives away her money and a marble to others. Later they help her escape from the city as the gate is closed. When she reaches home, she realizes her home is her kingdom.

China is a very large country. Because of its size, many of its citizens live in contrasting environments. It is warm in southern China and these Chinese dress differently and eat different food from those in Northern China.

A. These words tell about Mei Li's Peking. What others can you add?

Great Wall	jugglers	lanterns
camels	peddlers	dragons
chopsticks	priests	city gate
firecrackers	rickshaws	fish kites
Kitchen God	ice sled	bandits
stilt walkers	canal	fortune sticks

_____   _____   _____

_____   _____   _____

B. Circle the words that name people.

C. Box the words that name places.

D. Underline the words that name things.

E. What is the most unusual thing you've named? _____

F. Which thing would you most like to see? _____

G. Which thing would you like to own the most? _____

   Why? _____

   _____

ENCYCLOPEDIA

DIRECTIONS: Find the title in the card catalog. Fill in the author's last name.

ACROSS
1. Dorrie and the Fortune Teller
2. A Woggle of Witches
3. Bed Knob and Broomstick
4. The Witch Family
5. The Fearsome Inn
6. Georgie's Halloween
7. Little Witch

DOWN
1. The Hairy Horror Trick
2. Jennifer, Hecate, Macbeth, William McKinley, and me, Elizabeth
3. A Ghost Named Fred
4. The Witches of Worm
5. The Ghost in the Noonday Sun
6. Whistle in the Graveyard

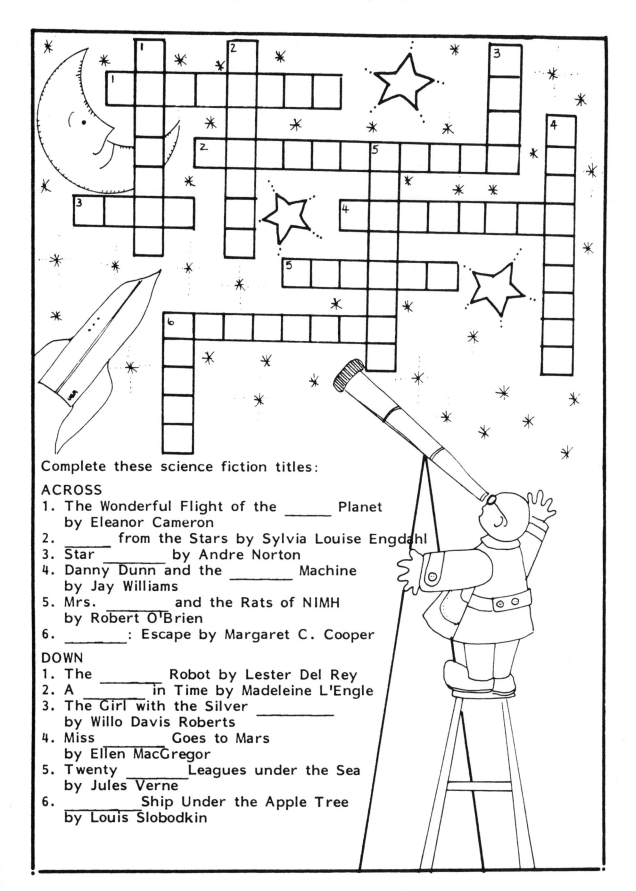

Complete these science fiction titles:

ACROSS
1. The Wonderful Flight of the _____ Planet
   by Eleanor Cameron
2. _____ from the Stars by Sylvia Louise Engdahl
3. Star _____ by Andre Norton
4. Danny Dunn and the _____ Machine
   by Jay Williams
5. Mrs. _____ and the Rats of NIMH
   by Robert O'Brien
6. _____: Escape by Margaret C. Cooper

DOWN
1. The _____ Robot by Lester Del Rey
2. A _____ in Time by Madeleine L'Engle
3. The Girl with the Silver _____
   by Willo Davis Roberts
4. Miss _____ Goes to Mars
   by Ellen MacGregor
5. Twenty _____ Leagues under the Sea
   by Jules Verne
6. _____ Ship Under the Apple Tree
   by Louis Slobodkin

BAFFLING BATTLES

Fill in the blanks with the subject that matches these Dewey Decimal numbers.

The United States has been involved in many wars during its history. The _____355.8 used in battles have changed. At one time, soldiers travelled on foot or by _____636.1. Later the _____385 made it easier to transport soldiers and supplies. Another development was _____387.2 and the _____359.3. _____629.13 caused major changes in the way battles were fought.

Early in our country's history, the _____914.4 and _____970.1 fought England.

In the _____973.3, we fought _____914.2.

During _____973.7, Americans fought against other Americans. In border states, like _____917.69 sometimes neighbors fought each other. One of the things that caused this was was _____326.

_____940.3 was supposed to make the "world safe for democracy." The Central Powers - _____914.3, _____914.36, _____914.39, _____914.977, and _____915.61, fought the Allies - _____914.2, _____914.4, _____914.7, _____914.5, and _____914.93, and the _____917.3.

War came again when _____914.3 invaded _____914.38.

The United States entered _____940.54 after _____915.2 attacked Pearl Harbor.

The _____341.23 was formed to help prevent future wars, but there have been wars since _____529 began.

CREATE YOUR OWN DEWEY DECIMAL STORY FOR OTHERS TO COMPLETE!

Dewey Decimal System Exercise

MYTHOLOGY MYSTERY

Fill in the blanks with the subject that matches these Dewey Decimal numbers.

Jason, Midas, Hercules, and Pan are all characters from _____292. The ancient people of _____938 and _____937 believed that gods and goddesses controlled _____551.5 and _____525. They believed they ruled the _____523.8 and _____523.4

Daedalus built _____728 and temples. After he had built a house for King Minos, Daedalus and his son Icarus were locked in a tower. They decided to escape by _____629.132. They gathered feathers from many _____598.2 to make wings. Their wings worked so well that Icarus flew too near the _____523.7. He fell into the sea and was never seen again.

King Midas was granted his wish that everything he touched would turn to gold. He walked in his garden, and the _____581 turned to gold when he touched them. His serious problems began when he discovered his _____641.3 turned to gold.

Pan was the god of _____780. He was half-goat, half man.

Hercules was very strong, and had adventures called the "Twelve Labors of Hercules." He had to kill a lion and the Hydra, which was like a _____598.1 with nine heads and nine necks. Another task was to tame a pair of _____636.1. Hercules also had to go to the underworld to get Cerberus, a three-headed _____636.7 with a dragon's tail.

CREATE YOUR OWN DEWEY DECIMAL MYSTERY FOR OTHERS TO SOLVE!

USING REFERENCE SOURCES

I. BIOGRAPHICAL DICTIONARIES

Select ten people who are or were outstanding in one field (artists, inventors, sports figures etc.). Develop a chart of basic information about them. What elements were common in their lives? What conclusions can you draw?

born in city					
born in country					
wealthy family					
much education					

II. FAMOUS FIRST FACTS

Select a product that interests you. Prepare a bulletin board display entitled FIRSTS IN _____. For example your display might center on FIRSTS IN motorcycles, watches, tires, etc.

III. ATLAS

A) Prepare a series of bulletins on lost ships or planes. Give the longitude and latitude of the ship or plane's last reported position. Challenge classmates to locate the missing ship or plane on a map.

B) Locate the following on the maps that follow. Use the index to the atlas for help.

Movie Monsters!

1. Godzilla (Japan)
2. Abominable Snowman (Himalayas)
3. The Mummy (Egypt)
4. Loch Ness Monster (Scotland)
5. Hydra (Greece)
6. Moa (New Zealand
7. Dracula (Transylvania)
8. The Fly (Eastern Canada)
9. Jaws (Long Island Coast)
10. Bigfoot (American Northwest)
11. The Tarantula (Southwestern U.S.)
12. Creature from the Black Lagoon (Amazon jungle)

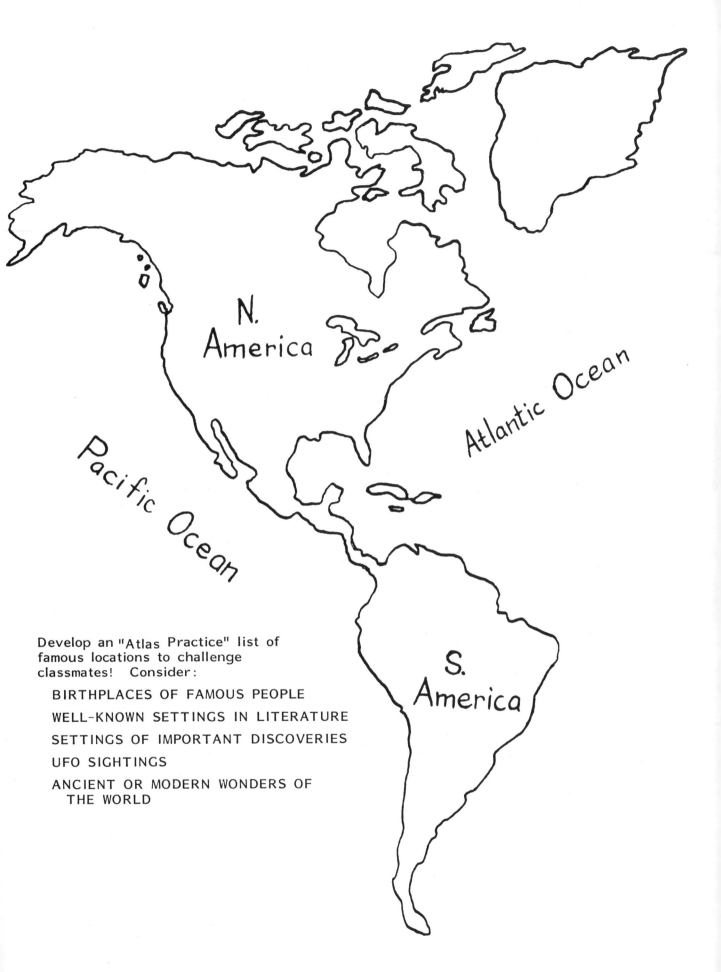

N.
America

Atlantic Ocean

Pacific Ocean

S.
America

Develop an "Atlas Practice" list of
famous locations to challenge
classmates! Consider:

BIRTHPLACES OF FAMOUS PEOPLE

WELL-KNOWN SETTINGS IN LITERATURE

SETTINGS OF IMPORTANT DISCOVERIES

UFO SIGHTINGS

ANCIENT OR MODERN WONDERS OF
   THE WORLD

Kane.   FAMOUS FIRST FACTS

> Interesting information about "firsts" in people, places and products in the United States.

Guinness.   BOOK OF WORLD RECORDS

> Interesting information about records...longest, shortest, lowest, highest, largest etc. Refers to worldwide records.

Brewer.   DICTIONARY OF PHRASE AND FABLE

> Dictionary arrangement of phrases and terms with definition or literature reference.

Bartlett.   FAMILIAR QUOTATIONS

> Guide to familiar quotations through use of a key word index which leads to the page on which the quote is given. Chronological arrangement by author.

WHERE WOULD YOU LOOK?

1. What was the size of the largest pizza ever made? _____

2. Where was the first ice cream cone made? _____

3. What is meant by "to wear the willow?" _____

4. What does abracadabra mean? _____

5. Who said "Give me liberty or give me death"? _____

6. What was the date on which the statement "The only thing we have to fear is fear itself" was made? _____

7. What was the length of the longest mustache ever grown? _____

8. If someone said "Oh horsefeathers" what would he/she mean? _____

9. In what state was the first library established? _____

10. Look in Bartlett's Quotations. Find one quote that you feel is worth remembering. Share the quote in an original way with classmates.

11. After browsing through Famous First Facts decide what "Firsts" can still be accomplished. List three.

12. If you could be remembered in Bartlett's for something you have said, what would it be?

13. If you were cited in the Guinness Book Of World Records, what would you like to be cited for?

14. What modern phrase does not appear in Brewer's Dictionary that you predict will appear in the next edition?

A. DIRECTIONS:
Place an X on each state mentioned by name in the letter. Place a O in each state INFERRED but not specifically mentioned by name. For example: The Rio Grande is in what state? Be prepared to prove your answers.

Letter From A Trucker

Dear Mom,

What a way to see the country! I started out in California on US 101 and drove it all the way to the Canadian border. Then I turned tail and headed east. I followed the whole Oregon trail and camped one night in a redwood stand. I watched Old Faithful do its thing, then headed south and crossed the Rio Grande twice. On the way south I stopped at the ghost town named Jerome, built right on the side of a mountain!

I followed the Santa Fe trail east its whole length and had lunch under the Gateway Arch. You wouldn't believe the mountains in this country! I've climbed the Blue Mountains, White Mountains, Rockies, Ozarks, and Applachians and the Smokies! The Empire State Building seemed higher than some of those mountains though! I drove the whole gulf coast and had my only trouble when my truck broke down in a tobacco field.

I'm heading home now and just passed through the Dells after bypassing Lake Michigan.

It will be great to get home to hog country again!

R
E
F
E
R
E
N
C
E

ALMANAC PRACTICE

Use an almanac, found in the reference section of the library, to answer these questions about monsters and the movies.

A. Movie Monsters

1. Who actually invented movies so that monsters could be seen life-like and in action? _____

2. How long have movies had spoken dialogue so that movie-goers could hear monsters cry and speak? _____

3. Where was "the man of a thousand faces", Lon Chaney, born and when? _____ _____ _____

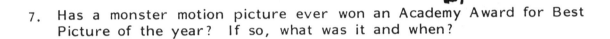

4. What was Boris Karloff's real name? _____

5. What was Bela Lugosi's real name? _____

6. Where was Bela Lugosi's birthplace? _____

7. Has a monster motion picture ever won an Academy Award for Best Picture of the year? If so, what was it and when? _____

8. One of these monster film actors (Frederic March, Lon Chaney, Vincent Price) once won an Academy Award for Best Actor but had to share the honor with another actor, as that year there was a tie vote. Which actor was it? _____

9. With whom did this monster actor tie for Best Actor of the Year? And what was the motion picture he played in to win the award? _____ _____

B. Select a topic of interest to you. Using the almanac, develop ten questions on your topic for others to answer.

C. Using the almanac, develop ten additional questions which have numbers as answers (weight, distance, dates, amounts, etc.). Develop a math game similar to the Reference Math Activity found in this section. Example:

1. Add the height of the Empire State Building _____

2. To the date Missouri was admitted to the Union _____

3. Subtract the height of the Gateway Arch _____

RHODE ISLAND

RESEARCHING THE FIFTY STATES

Choose one state you would like to know more about. Research and complete the activities listed below.

PEOPLE

1. What generalization is made about people from this state? Find evidence to prove or disprove it!

FOOD

2. The President is coming to dinner ! Plan a menu using only food and ingredients grown or produced in your state.

LANDFORMS

3. What is the most important landform in your state? What effects would be felt in this state if this landform disappeared?

INDUSTRY

4. What (and where) are the two largest industries in your state? What might cause these industries to move to another state? What would be the effect if these industries left your state? How can more industry be attracted to your state?

LAW

5. Using the correct form, write your own bill for a law you would like to see passed in your state.

TOURISM

6. Where in your state did a famous historical event take place? How could this place be made a historical site that tourists would like to visit?

7. **CAPITOL**

If the capitol building were moved to another part of your state who would be affected and how?

REFERENCE SOURCE QUICK CHECK

Reference books are kept together in one section labeled "Reference". You will use these books often to answer many questions. Each reference book has a special purpose:

1. ATLAS - A book of maps and charts
2. ALMANAC - A book published every year that gives current facts on many subjects.
3. DICTIONARY - A book that gives the spelling, pronunciation, and definition of words.
4. ENCYCLOPEDIAS - A set of books that gives general information on many topics. Topics are arranged in alphabetical order.
5. BIOGRAPHICAL DICTIONARY - A dictionary of famous people.
6. GEOGRAPHICAL DICTIONARY - A dictionary of cities and countries of the world.
7. DICTIONARY OF SYNONYMS - A dictionary of words that have similar meanings.
8. READER'S GUIDE - A book of magazine topics listed in alphabetical order.

Answers are often found in more than one reference book. To save time, it is important to know the BEST SOURCE. The best source is the book MOST LIKELY to contain the answer you want to find.

Read each question below. Write the name of the reference book that is the BEST SOURCE to use.

1. What is the current world population of whooping cranes? _____

2. Who was John Muir? _____

3. What is another word meaning conservation? _____

4. When was Theodore Roosevelt born? _____

5. Where are U. S. National Parks located? _____

6. How many mammals were on the endangered species list in 1978? _____

7. What are some major U.S. programs in the field of conservation? _____

8. Where can you find a map of Canada? _____

9. What current magazines have articles on endangered species? _____

10. How many words have the same meaning as endanger? _____

11. What are some places of interest in Wyoming? _____

12. What are the best highways between Boise, Idaho and Odgen, Utah? _____

    _____

13. How do you pronounce the word "species"? _____

14. How many major forest fires were there in the U.S. in 1977? _____

RESEARCH
ACTIVITIES 1-3

GUIDELINES

Research activities for primary children are largely teacher selected. Best activities are HANDS ON experiences.

Students learn about and relate information by interacting with the material. Independent learning centers are often used.

Beginning book research should stress the use of the child's SKILLS OF OBSERVATION.

Picture books can serve as good beginning research vehicles.

For individual interests, prepare research cards similar to those included in this section.

ACTIVITIES IN THIS SECTION ARE:

1. Hands-on observational activities.

2. Observational research using books.

3. Picture book research requiring reading skills.

4. Research requiring beginning reference tools: dictionary and encyclopedia.

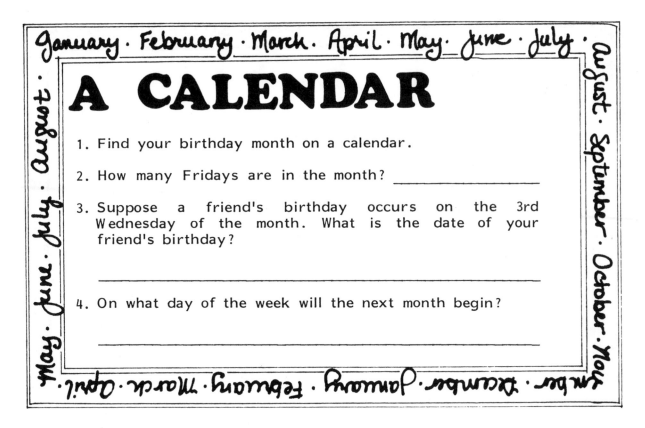

January · February · March · April · May · June · July ·

A CALENDAR

1. Find your birthday month on a calendar.

2. How many Fridays are in the month? _____

3. Suppose a friend's birthday occurs on the 3rd Wednesday of the month. What is the date of your friend's birthday?

   _____

4. On what day of the week will the next month begin?

   _____

HAIR

snake · bear · duck · cow · fish · horse · rabbit

1. How many girls in your class have long hair? _____ Short hair? _____

2. Is long or short hair more popular in your class? _____

3. Circle the names of animals that have hair or fur.

snake	cow	rabbit	turtle
bear	fish	lizard	fox
duck	horse	chicken	armadillo

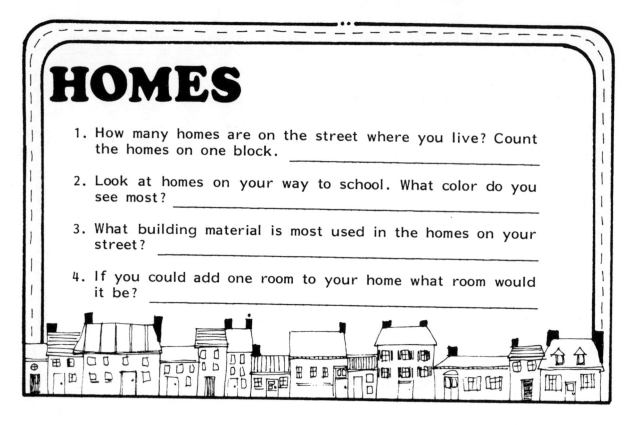

HOMES

1. How many homes are on the street where you live? Count the homes on one block. _____

2. Look at homes on your way to school. What color do you see most? _____

3. What building material is most used in the homes on your street? _____

4. If you could add one room to your home what room would it be? _____

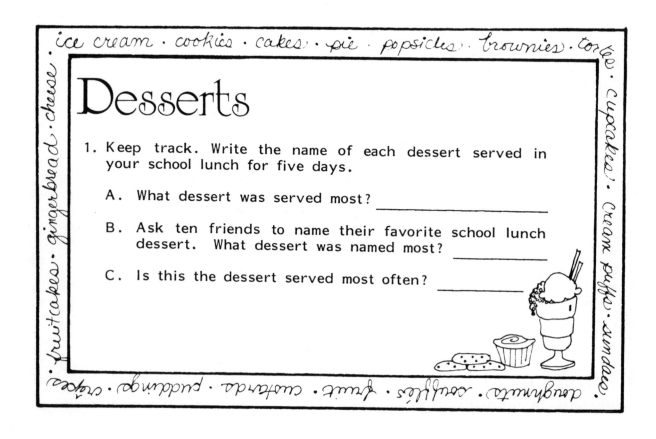

Desserts

1. Keep track. Write the name of each dessert served in your school lunch for five days.

   A. What dessert was served most? _____

   B. Ask ten friends to name their favorite school lunch dessert. What dessert was named most? _____

   C. Is this the dessert served most often? _____

A Soda Straw

1. Name three things you can drink with a straw.

    _____   _____   _____

2. Name one other thing you could do with a straw. _____

3. Divide 12 soda straws into two groups. How many different groups can you make? _____

4. Create something new with your twelve soda straws.

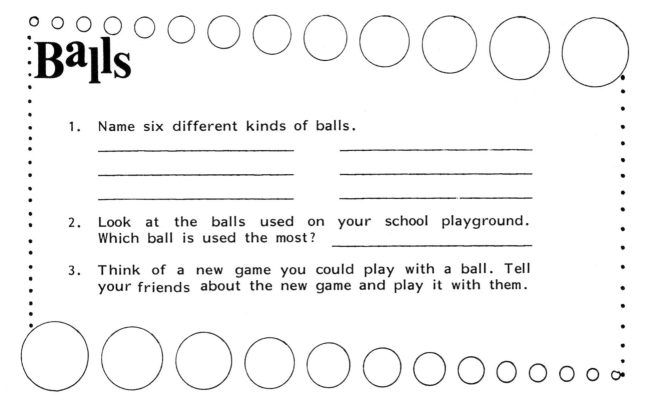

Balls

1. Name six different kinds of balls.

    _____   _____

    _____   _____

    _____   _____

2. Look at the balls used on your school playground. Which ball is used the most? _____

3. Think of a new game you could play with a ball. Tell your friends about the new game and play it with them.

POTATOES · POTATOES · POTATOES · POTATOES · POTATOES · POTATOES · POTA

potatoes

1. At what temperature would you bake a potato for one hour? _____ degrees

   How can you find out if you are right? _____

2. Do potatoes have seeds? _____

3. Name as many ways as you can to eat potatoes:

"one potato, two potato, three potato, four, five potato, six potato, seven potato, more"

SHOES

1. How many different kinds of shoes can you name?

2. What can you do with a shoestring besides tie your shoe? _____

3. Complete the patterns on these shoestrings.

00 X 00 X

0000 oo 00 o 0000

apples · oranges · coconuts · grapes · blueberries · strawberries · bananas · Cantalope · watermelon · pears

LEARNING ABOUT APPLES

OBSERVE THREE APPLES CUT IN HALF

1. Remove the seeds from one apple (two halves). How many seeds does it have? _____

2. Do all apples have the same number of seeds? _____

3. How can you find out?

   _____

4. Were you right? _____

5. Tell three ways an apple is like a banana.

   _____

   _____

   _____

6. Tell three ways an apple is like a stoplight.

   _____

   _____

   _____

7. List things you might see if you built a treehouse in an apple tree.

   _____

   _____

   _____ _____

8. Divide a set of eight apples into as many different groups as you can. How many groups did you make? _____

watermelon · cantalope · bananas · strawberries · blueberries · grapes

peaches · apricots · apples · oranges · coconuts

LOOKING AROUND OUR SCHOOL

1. How many children are in your class?

2. How many children are in each of three other classes in your school?   (1) _____   (2) _____   (3) _____

3. Do all classes have the same number of students? _____

4. Observe the playground at recess.

   Where do the boys play most?   _____

   Where do the girls play most?   _____

   Are there more boys or girls on the playground?   _____

5. Name living things you see on the playground that are not children.

   _____   _____

   _____   _____

6. Name one way your playground could be made a better place to play.

   _____

7. Observe the teachers in your school. How many are men? _____ How many are women? _____ Do men teach more upper grade classes or lower grade classes? _____

8. Take a survey. Ask twenty students what time each would like school to start. Record the answers. What answer appears most often? Report your results to the school principal.

   Most students feel that school should start at _____ o'clock.

WINDOWS AND DOORS

1. How many windows are in your house? _____

2. How many windows are in your classroom? _____

3. Take a survey: CHECK AND COUNT
   How many doors you can find in your school building? _____

   How many of these doors lead outside? _____

   How many of these doors have a window in them? _____

   Do most doors open into a room or away from a room? _____

4. How many different kinds of doors can you think of?

   _____

   _____

   _____

   _____

   _____

5. If you could open a door and enter a very special place, what
   place would it be?

   _____

A BOOK OF NON FICTION GIVES FACTUAL INFORMATION ON A TOPIC.

FIND A BOOK ABOUT

ANSWER THESE QUESTIONS

Alligators

1. Name one enemy of the alligator.

_____

2. Why do alligators NOT live in Alaska?

_____

_____

Brain

1. How many parts does your brain have?

_____

2. What does your brain let you do that animals cannot do?

_____

_____

Caves

1. What rock formations hang from the ceiling of some caves?

_____

2. What would be the most important thing for you to take into a cave?

_____

Dinosaurs

1. What was the biggest dinosaur?

_____

2. How do we know what dinosaurs look like?

_____

_____

FIND A BOOK ABOUT	ANSWER THESE QUESTIONS
**Eskimos**	1. Where do Eskimos live? _____ 2. Name one thing an Eskimo child your age can do that you cannot do. _____
Forest	1. Name two kinds of trees found in a forest. _____ _____ 2. What is the greatest danger to a forest? _____
Glaciers	1. What color are glaciers? _____ 2. Can people walk on glaciers? Why or why not? _____ _____
Horses	1. Name two kinds of horses. _____ 2. Which is smarter, a horse or a dog? _____

FIND A BOOK ABOUT	ANSWER THESE QUESTIONS

Insects

1. How many legs does an insect have? _____

2. How many legs does a spider have? _____

3. Is a spider an insect? _____ Why or why not? _____

Jungles

1. Name three jungle animals. _____ _____ _____

2. Why are jungles so thick with plants and trees? _____

Kangaroos

1. Where do kangaroos live? _____

2. Why do you think a mother kangaroo has a pocket and a mother rabbit does not? _____

Lighthouses

1. Why do lighthouses exist? _____

2. What does a lighthouse keeper do? _____

FIND A BOOK ABOUT	ANSWER THESE QUESTIONS

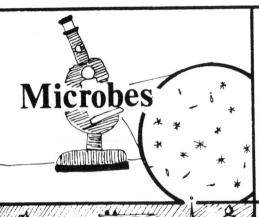

Microbes

1. Where can you see microbes?

_____

2. Name one good thing microbes do?

_____

_____

New York City

1. Where is New York City located?

_____

2. Name two famous places you would like to visit in New York City.

_____

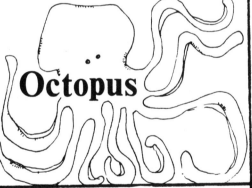

Octopus

1. How many legs does an octopus have? _____

2. Name two places you could go to see an octopus.

_____

_____

Pigs

1. Are all pigs pink? How can you prove your answer?

2. Would a pig make a good pet? Why or why not?

FIND A BOOK ABOUT	ANSWER THESE QUESTIONS

Queens

1. What is a Queen?
_____

2. Name a fairy tale Queen.
_____

3. Name a Queen living today.
_____

Robots

1. Name two things robots can do.
_____
_____

2. If you had a robot, what would you have it do?
_____
_____

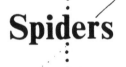

Spiders

1. What do spiders eat?
_____

2. Why does a spider make a web?
_____
_____

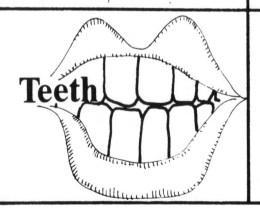

Teeth

1. About when does a human baby get its first tooth?
_____

2. How do people lose their teeth?
_____
_____

FIND A BOOK ABOUT	ANSWER THESE QUESTIONS

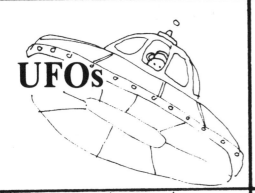

UFOs

1. What does U.F.O. mean?

_____

2. If you saw a U.F.O., what would you do?

_____

_____

Volcanoes

1. Name a city that was covered by volcanic ash.

_____

2. Could your city be covered by volcanic ash? _____

3. Why or why not?

_____

Whales

1. How do we know a whale is not a fish?

_____

2. How much can a large whale weigh? _____

3. What do whales eat?

_____

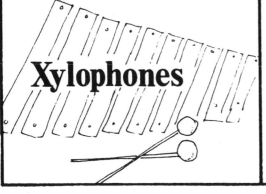

Xylophones

1. What are xylophone bars made of? _____

2. What would you hold in your hand in order to play the xylophone? _____

3. Why do the bars on a xylophone make different sounds? _____

FIND A BOOK ABOUT	ANSWER THESE QUESTIONS

A Yard

1. How long is a yard in feet?

   In inches? _____
   _____

2. Name things we buy by the yard.

   _____

   _____

Zebras

1. In what country are zebras found running wild?

   _____

2. How fast can a zebra run?

   _____

3. What other animal might you see near a wild zebra?

   _____

NOW THAT YOU HAVE SUCCESSFULLY COMPLETED THIS ABC RESEARCH PROJECT, WRITE YOUR OWN ABCs OF RESEARCH FOR SOMEONE ELSE TO SOLVE.

"now I know my ABC's..."

Ocean Creatures

Name of ocean creature _____.

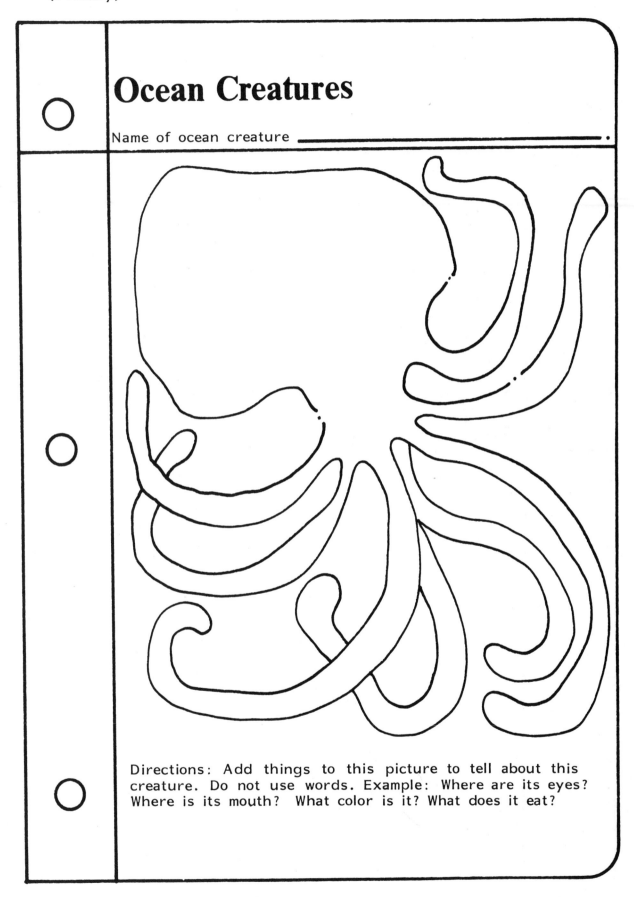

Directions: Add things to this picture to tell about this creature. Do not use words. Example: Where are its eyes? Where is its mouth? What color is it? What does it eat?

Insects

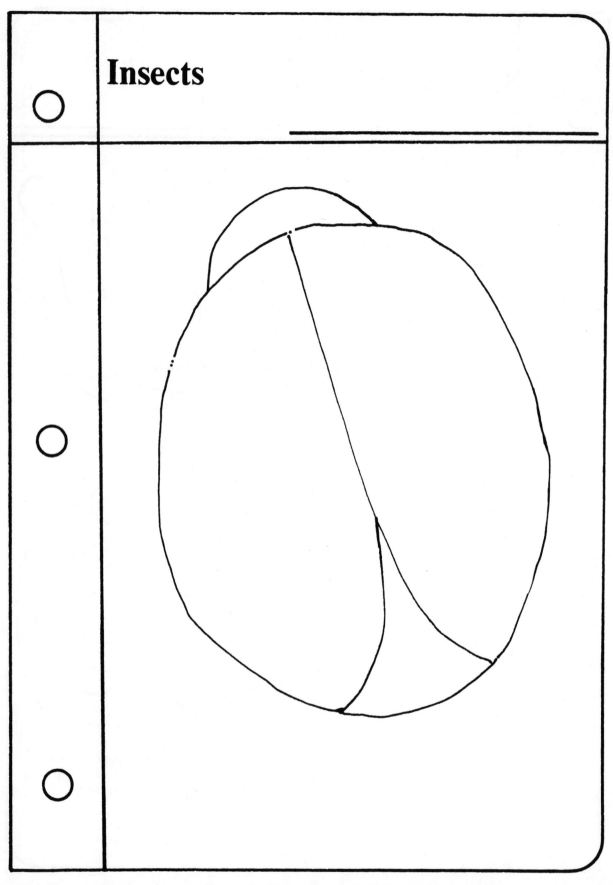

ADD THINGS TO THIS PICTURE TO TELL ABOUT THIS INSECT.

Birds

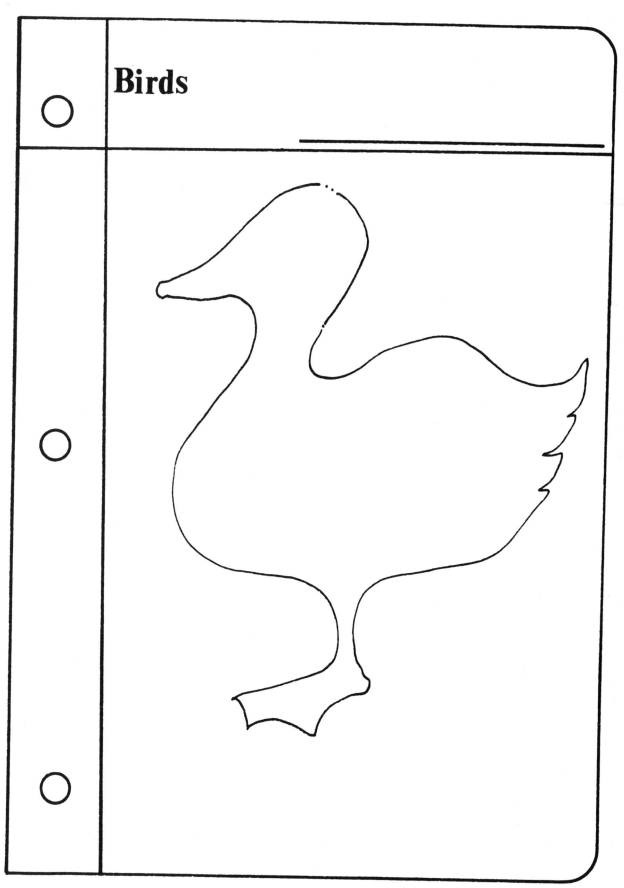

ADD THINGS TO THIS PICTURE TO TELL ABOUT THIS BIRD.

Community Helpers

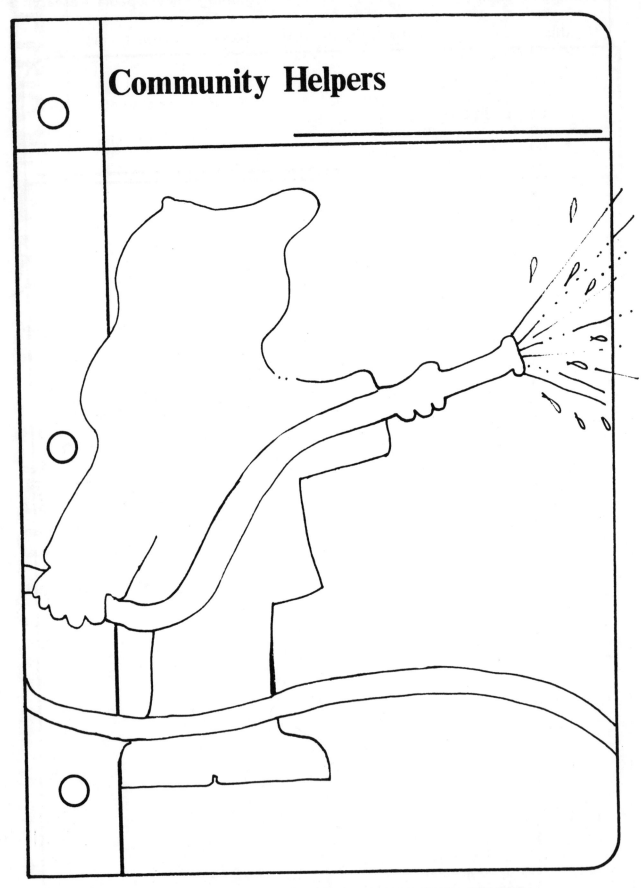

ADD THINGS TO THIS PICTURE TO TELL ABOUT THIS HELPER

Aliki, B.   DIGGING UP DINOSAURS   Crowell, 1981

A. Making a dinosaur exhibit is almost like working a puzzle. Write about what has to be done by writing what comes first, second, and so on.
B. Look at all the different people who help dig up dinosaurs on page 14 and 15. Write the name of the kind of helper you would like to be and tell why you would like to do this.

Aliki, B.   WILD AND WOOLLY MAMMOTHS

Crowell, 1977

A. How do scientists know what the woolly mammoth looked like? Write a sentence and draw a picture about it.
B. Make a picture and write a sentence telling some things we know about mammoth hunters.
C. Can you make a list of ways the mammoth hunters used the woolly mammoth?
D. Do you think we may see a woolly mammoth? Why or why not?

Anderson, Lucia   THE SMALLEST LIFE AROUND US

Crown Publ. 1978

A. Microbes can grow by getting so big they split in half and make two microbes. If you could split in half and grow into another person, you would have a twin exactly like yourself. Give your twin a name and tell about her or him.
B. How could you grow some microbes so you could look at them more closely? Write a plan for growing microbes.
C. Some microbes are good and some are bad. Choose good microbes or bad microbes. Write about what these microbes can do.

RESEARCH CARDS

1-3

Branley, Franklyn M. <u>OXYGEN</u> <u>KEEPS</u> <u>YOU</u> <u>ALIVE</u>

Crowell, 1971

A. Make a list of places people go where they have to take oxygen with them in order to stay alive.
B. Make a drawing showing how man, fish and leaves get oxygen from the air. Label the parts you have drawn.

Branley, Franklyn M. <u>THE</u> <u>PLANETS</u> <u>IN</u> <u>OUR</u> <u>SOLAR</u> <u>SYSTEM</u>

Crowell, 1981

A. The sun and the nine planets are in space. Make a list of some other objects in space. Make a picture to show what the objects on your list look like.
B. If the planets were going to have a race to see who could go around the sun the fastest, who would win?
C. If it were possible for people to live on another planet, which one would you choose?

Carmichael, Carrie <u>BIGFOOT</u>: <u>MAN</u>, <u>MONSTER</u> <u>OR</u> <u>MYTH</u>

Raintree , 1977

A. Do you believe any of the stories about bigfoot are true? Write about what you believe. Be sure to tell why you believe this way.
B. Why do you think the monster you read about is called Bigfoot? Write some reasons for this name being used to describe the monster.
C. Some people do not believe there is such a monster. Write some reasons why they think there is no Bigfoot monster.

1-3

Cecil, George   SALT   Franklin Watts, 1976

A. Why do you think salt shakers were made so fancy a long
    time ago?
B. Can you write about some ways we get salt to use today?
C. Make a list of things salt is used for.

Cobb, Vicki   LOTS OF ROT   Lippencott, 1981

A. Pretend you are a scientist. Make a list of rules to stop
    mold and bacteria from growing on food.
B. By reading this book do you find any good reasons why a
    bulldozer covers things taken to the city dump with dirt?
    Write some reasons.
C. Can you list any good things about rot?
D. Make up an experiment you think would work about rot
    that you did not read about in this book.

Cole, Joanna   DINOSAUR STORY   Wm.Morrow & Co. 1974

A. Make a time line showing when the different kinds of
    dinosaurs lived.
B. How do scientists know about dinosaurs? Tell how you
    think they learned so much about them.
C. If you were lucky enough to find a dinosaur bone, what
    would you do with it? Tell about the kind it is and where
    you will put it.

1-3

Conklin, Gladys   I CAUGHT A LIZARD

Holiday House, 1967

A. Which of the animals in this book would you like to have? Why? Find out five things about that animal and write them as well as your reasons for wanting that particular animal.
B. How do you feel about the way the boy treated these animals? Write about your feelings, and give reasons or examples from the book to support your point of view.
C. If you have had a pet, at least for a short time, write a story about it.

Freedman, Russell   TOOTH AND CLAW: A Look at Animal Weapons

Holiday House, 1980

A. Choose one animal in this book which you think has an interesting way to get food. Write about this animal.
B. You read about many animal weapons in this book. Which animal do you think has the most dangerous weapon for protecting itself? Write about it.
C. Make a list of facts about animals you did not know before reading this book.

Gans, Roma   CAVES   Crowell, 1976

A. Pretend that you have discovered a cave. Make a map of the rooms in the cave so visitors can explore the cave. Give each of the rooms a name.
B. There are some unusual things inside caves. Can you draw and list some of the things which you think are unusual?

1-3

Gans, Roma   ICEBERGS   Crowell, 1964

A. What do you think ship captains should know about icebergs? Write a sentence and make a picture about it.
B. Is there anything good about icebergs? Write a sentence and make a picture about it.
C. Where do icebergs come from? Draw a globe shape of the earth and put red O on places where icebergs start.

Gemme, Leila B.   THE MARS LANDING

Children's Press, 1977

A. Why was the invention of the telescope important? Write about it. Make a picture of what you might see if you looked through a telescope.
B. Do you think people live on Mars? Tell why or why not.
C. If you had been on Viking I or Viking II, where would you have gone? What would you have seen?

Goldreich, Gloria   WHAT CAN SHE BE? A SCIENTIST

Holt, Rinehart, & Winston, 1981

A. This book says a scientist is like a detective. Write about how these two people are alike.
B. If you could choose a new discovery for Dr. Sharon to make about medicine, what would it be? Write about how this discovery would help people.
C. Would you like to be a scientist someday? Write about what you may choose to be when you are grown up.

RESEARCH CARDS

1-3

Gregory, Olive Barnes   COCOA AND CHOCOLATE

Rourke Publ. 1981

A. Make a picture story showing where a chocolate bar comes
   from. Begin with a seed being planted in the ground.
B. If you could invent a new delicious food made from
   chocolate, what would it be? Make a picture of it and
   write an advertisement for it.

Grosvenor, Donna K.   ZOO BABIES   National Geographic
                                         Society, 1978

A. Choose one animal from this book that you think does
   something unusual. Write about what makes this animal
   unusual and make a picture of it.
B. Of all the zoo workers, which one would you most like to
   be? Tell why.
C. Do you think being in a zoo is good or bad for animals?
   Tell why.

Harris, Susan   CREATURES WITH POCKETS

Franklin Watts, 1980

A. Which animal in this book is the most interesting to you?
   Tell why and make a picture of it.
B. If something should happen to the mother animal soon
   after her baby was born, what do you think would
   happen to the baby? Write about it.
C. Why do you think these animals all have pockets while
   most animals do not? List some reasons.

Harris, Susan.   <u>VOLCANOES</u>   Franklin Watts, 1979

A. Did you read about the two cities which were covered by volcanic ash about 2000 years ago? Do you think your city will ever be covered with ash from a volcano? Write about why or why not.
B. If you lived near a volcano and had to leave your home, what things would you choose to take with you? Make a list.
C. Three volcanoes have erupted in the United States since this book was written. (two in Hawaii, named Mauna Loa and Kilanea, and Mount St. Helens in Washington). Write a list of questions for our group to discuss about these volcanoes.

Harris, Susan.   <u>WHALES</u>   Franklin Watts, 1980

A. This book says there soon may be no whales left. Write about what man can do to save the whales from all dying out.
B. Make a list of facts which help us know that whales are not just fish.
C. Write some facts about the whale you found the most interesting. Make a picture to show what this whale looks like.

Harris, Susan   <u>THE WORLD BENEATH THE SEA</u>

Franklin Watts, 1979

A. If you could be a diver, what would you like to look for and learn about in the sea? Write about being a diver.
B. There are things other than plants and animals which can be found in the sea or ocean. Make a list of other things in the ocean.
C. Would you like to be in a sealab or a submarine? Write about why or why not.
D. Choose one interesting animal who lives in the ocean. Write about why this animal is unusual.

RESEARCH CARDS

1-3

Harris, Susan   UNIDENTIFIED FLYING OBJECTS

Franklin Watts, 1980

A. Why do you think scientists do not believe the stories that people tell about seeing and talking to creatures from outer space? List some reasons.
B. Do you believe there really were UFO's? Write about what you think the UFO's seen really might be.
C. What facts really make some people believe that there are UFO's from other planets near our earth?

Hill, Mary Lou   MY DAD'S A PARK RANGER

Children's Press, 1977

A. An animal in this book gets to go for a helicopter ride. Tell where it is going and why it is going there.
B. Why do you think national parks have Rangers? List some reasons.
C. Have you ever been to a national park? Write about what you saw and make a map showing where it is.

James, Harry Clebourne   THE FIRST AMERICANS

Elk Grove Press, 1971

A. Can you make a drawing of one kind of Indian home and write a sentence about it?
B. What are some things we have today that Indian children did not have?
C. Some Indians used to live in caves. Write about why you think it was a good idea for Indians to live in a cave.

1-3

Jaspersohn, William   <u>HOW</u> <u>THE</u> <u>FOREST</u> <u>GREW</u>

Greenwillow Books, 1980

A. Make a time line showing how the forest started and changed.
B. A forest has many trees and many other living things. Make a picture of some other things which live in the forest. Write some sentences about the things you would like to see.
C. This book has a list of rules about things you <u>should</u> <u>not</u> do in the forest. Can you make a list of things you <u>can</u> do in the forest?

Kleiner, Art   <u>A</u> <u>LOOK</u> <u>INSIDE</u> <u>ROBOTS</u>

Raintree Pub. , 1981

A. List some interesting things real robots can do. On the back of your paper, make a list of things you can think of that real robots cannot do.
B. Make a picture of a robot you would like to build. It can be real, like the Disneyland and Disney World robots or it can be like the robots in Star Wars. Write some things your robot can do.
C. Pretend that you could have a robot who comes to school with you. Make a list of all the things you want your robot to do for you at school.

Lauber, Patricia   <u>MYSTERY</u> <u>MONSTERS</u> <u>OF</u> <u>LOCH</u> <u>NESS</u>

Garrard   Pub., 1978

A. Do you think the Loch Ness Monster (if there is any) is a mammal, a fish, a mollusk, a reptile or an amphibian? Circle your answer. Then write why you think this way.
B. Choose one of the animal groups told about in this book. Circle your choice: mammal reptile amphibian fish mollusk. Make a picture showing what these kinds of animals are like. Write some facts about your picture.

1-3

Morris, Robert A.   <u>SEAHORSE</u>   Harper & Row, 1972

A. How does a seahorse eat? Make a picture of a seahorse eating something - and write about how he does this.
B. Would you like to have eyes like a seahorse? Tell what you could do if you had seahorse eyes!
C. What does the male seahorse do that most other animals do not do? Write about it.

Pluchrose, Henry   <u>ESKIMOS</u>   Gloucester, 1980

A. Make a drawing of a sledge, an umiak or kayak. Write a sentence about what your drawing was used for.
B. Choose one thing the Eskimos did which you think was the most unusual. Draw a picture and write some sentences about this unusual thing.
C. Would you like to be an Eskimo? Write about why you would or would not and make a picture about your reasons.

Podendorf, Illa   THE <u>T</u>RUE <u>B</u>OOK <u>O</u>F <u>J</u>UNGLES

Children's Press, 1959

A. Why do you think plants grow so well in a jungle? Write about it.
B. Can you draw some animals which live in the jungle? Write their names too.
C. What is the most interesting thing to you in the jungle? Make a picture and tell why it is the most interesting.
D. How does the jungle help us? Make a list.

Ryder, Joanne   <u>SNAIL</u> <u>IN</u> <u>THE</u> <u>WOODS</u>   Harper & Row, 1979

A. What kinds of animals are enemies of the snail? Make a picture of them and write their names.
B. What can the snail do with its feelers? Make a picture of the snail using its feelers and write about it.
C. Are there other animals you know about who have a shell? Make a list of them.

Selsam, Millicent Ellis   <u>GREG'S</u> <u>MICROSCOPE</u>

Harper & Row, 1963

A. Do you think the money Greg's father spent on a microscope was worth it? Tell why or why not.
B. Do you know some ways microscopes help us? Make a list.
C. What do you think was the most interesting thing Greg saw in his microscope? Write about why it was the most interesting and make a picture of it.

Shapp, Martha & Charles   <u>LET'S</u> <u>FIND</u> <u>OUT</u> <u>ABOUT</u> <u>THE</u> <u>MOON</u>

F. Watts, 1975

A. Make a list of things astronauts have found out about the moon.
B. Make a picture of a suit an astronaut has to wear to live on the moon. Tell why they have to wear special suits on the moon.
C. What do you think is the most interesting fact about the moon? Write about it.

RESEARCH CARDS

1-3

Shaw, Evelyn   ALLIGATOR   Harper & Row, 1972

A. Make a list of some enemies of the alligator.
B. In this story, man wanted to kill the alligator for her skin. Can you name some other animals useful to man and tell how they are used? (alligator=skin) Can you list more?

Shaw, Evelyn   OCTOPUS   Harper & Row, 1971

A. Can you make a list of true things about an octopus? Hint: eight legs
B. A baby octopus hatches from   an egg.   Some babies are born from their mothers' bodies. Can you name some of each kind?
C. Can you write a riddle about the octopus to see if your friends can guess what sea animal you are describing?

Simon, Seymour   ABOUT YOUR BRAIN   McGraw Hill, 1982

A. What is the smartest mammal in the world? Draw a picture of one of these mammals.
B. Make list of things your brain helps you do.
C. Make a picture of the brain and a picture of a computer. Which one is the smartest? Write why you think so.

RESEARCH CARDS

1-3

Tangborn, Wendell V.   <u>GLACIERS</u>   Crowell, 1965

A. Can you make up an invention which can stop glaciers from moving? Make a picture of it.
B. Make a time-line about glaciers. A time-line tells what happens first, second, third. Make pictures to show your time line.
C. Look at the map on page 28. Was your state covered by glaciers during the Ice Age? Make a map of your state showing the parts covered by glaciers.

Truby, David   <u>AUSTRALIA</u>   Watts, 1980

A. Pretend that you are going to spend Christmas in Australia. How would it be different from Christmas in your state?
B. Look at the map on page 9. Read about the different parts of Australia. Which part would you like to visit most? Tell why.
C. What one fact did you find the most interesting in this book? Tell why and make a picture about it.

Van Sickle, Sylvia, Ed.Con.   <u>POLLUTION</u>

Macdonald Educational, 1975

A. List some things man has done to cause pollution.
B. List some things man has done to help improve the pollution problem.
C. Which methods of travel do you think are less polluting than others? Make a picture of these ways of travel.

RESEARCH CARDS

1-3

Van Sickle, Sylvia, Ed.Con.   SIGNALS AND MESSAGES

Macdonald Educational, 1975

A. Choose one way messages can be sent. Write about why you think this is an interesting way to send messages.
B. Make some pictures which show how you get messages every day.
C. Make up a message you think is being sent by someone in this book. It can be a lighthouse message, smoke signal or any other.

Van Sickle, Sylvia, Ed.Con.   THE UNIVERSE

Macdonald Educational, 1975

A. Write a sentence telling why you would or would not like to live on Mars. Make a drawing of the space ship which helped us learn about Mars and write the name of this ship.
B. Choose one of the planets you are most interested in. Make a drawing of it and write some sentences which describe what this planet is like.
C. Imagine that it is a dark night and you can see a constellation (group of stars). Draw a picture of something a family of stars could show. Make the stars and draw lines between them to show your pictures.

Wonder Books.   SPIDERS   Grosset & Dunlap, 1974

A. Can you make a list of things which describe spiders?
B. What kind of spider do you think is the most interesting? Make a picture of it and tell why you think this spider is interesting.
C. Can you list some ways spiders are helpful and some ways spiders are harmful to us?
D. Which kind of web is the most interesting to you? Can you draw a web for us to see?

RESEARCH CARDS

1-3

Wonder Books.   THE SEA   Grossett & Dunlap, 1974

A. Do you know why the sea is salty? Write about this.
B. Make a picture about how man uses salt from the sea.
C. Many kinds of ships are in this book. Choose one kind you like and tell what this ship can do.
D. Pretend you are a diver. Make a picture about what you might see while you were under water.

Wonder Books.   TEETH   Grossett & Dunlap, 1972

A. Why do you think we have two different shapes of teeth? Write some sentences about it.
B. Make up a list of rules you think we should have about taking care of our teeth.
C. Have you lost any teeth? Write a story about how you lost a tooth and make a picture about it.

Wyler, Rose & Ames, Gerald   PROVE IT

Harper & Row, 1963

A. Tell what you have to do to prove an experiment. Why should you try it more than once?
B. Tell how you would prove to me that your throat vibrated.
C. List three things you found out that you didn't know before.

1-3

My Research Project

name

I WENT TO MY SCHOOL LIBRARY TO FIND OUT ABOUT

I SAW A

I LEARNED ABOUT

THIS IS A PICTURE OF

I THINK

SECTION FOUR

RESEARCH

ACTIVITIES 4-6

CONTENTS
1. Introducing the Research Process
2. Steps in the Research Process
3. Summary Sheet for Research Activity
4. Forms: Evaluation, Bibliography, Notetaking, Outlining
5. Research Cards: Short Projects to Stimulate Thinking
6. Researching Folktales
7. Creating a Mini-Newspaper
8. Animals in the News
9. Propaganda!
10. Learning About Gifted Persons

    A) Catnip Bill: A Story to Share
    B) Biography in Bloom (Using Bloom's Taxonomy for a Study of Biography)
    C) Researching the Lives of the Famous
    D) Researching Lives of Inventors
    E) Researching Artists, Actors, Authors

11. Photo Puzzlers
12. A Portmanteau of Products!

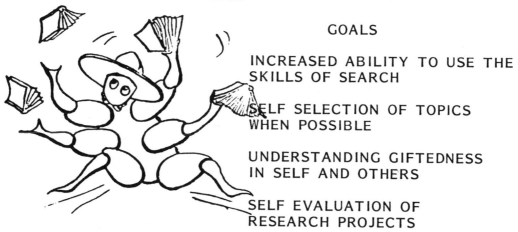

GOALS

INCREASED ABILITY TO USE THE SKILLS OF SEARCH

SELF SELECTION OF TOPICS WHEN POSSIBLE

UNDERSTANDING GIFTEDNESS IN SELF AND OTHERS

SELF EVALUATION OF RESEARCH PROJECTS

THE RESEARCH PROCESS

R. I. S. E.

Research and Independent Study Extravaganza

Today we live globally. Everything we do, and/or come in contact with, has global applications. Consider the following: hunger, weather, pollution, war. One could go on and on.

In order to allow students to be in touch with the fact that everything that is done today influences everything else worldwide, students must be given the opportunity to think about real problems, real events.

The students of today are the hope for the future. These are the people who will deal with future problems. They are the one who will devise new ways to solve them. They must become producers of ideas and not just consumers of knowledge. So the message to teachers and those who work with today's youth is this: think globally and act locally.

The teacher may not be the one who will preserve the future with a new solution to an age-old problem. But do not undermine the teacher's role. It is the teacher who must supply the student with the necessary skills to become a producer. These skills are part of the research process and are necessary for independent study to take place.

The aim here is to present for you, in a fanciful way, the steps in the research process. This process, when used in real life, enables a student to work on his/her own, to internalize a topic area, to produce a product, and to share his/her product with others--the step which often triggers or sends off ripples and brings back bigger and better approaches to solving problems.

Finally, some research projects are presented for your consideration. Some of these activities are multi-level. Some were used in enrichment programs and some were specifically used with students in a part-time gifted program. Sample forms used in the research process are provided. These may be used as they are presented here, or may be revised to fit an individual need or program.

Virginia T. Mealy
Resource Teacher/Librarian
St. Louis, Missouri

R.I.S.E. INTRODUCTION

A Story To Share With Young Researchers!

One day on the plains of central West Africa, Mambo, a large cow elephant, stopped foraging for food and went to consult the wise cow and the master bull who were the leaders of her herd. In simple language, Mambo related her concern about her first-born, Shani, a bull now nearly 12 years old.

Mambo explained that Shani did not seem to be learning the ways of the herd, so important to his survival. He was accident-prone because he daydreamed. He had been bitten by snakes three times because he was so foolishly trusting. Regardless of the discipline she used, Shani was a problem.

The wise leaders nodded in agreement. It was nearly noon. Noon in Africa is very hot. The sun shines like a gold coin in the sky. The wise leaders led Mambo to a cool, leafy place to rest. They were well aware of Shani and the problems he caused Mambo. More than once Shani had been a problem for them all when he had wandered away from the herd, when he had tried to swim when he was just a few weeks old, when his curiosity had gotten the best of him and he had fallen into a poacher's trap and had to be rescued by the herd. Oh, yes, Shani was one who stood apart from the others. He was a puzzlement and was certainly trying the patience of Mambo, as well as that of the wise leaders.

Mambo hung her head. It was a heartache for her to have a child who was so unpredictable and out-of-step with the herd.

"What's to become of him?" Mambo begged.

The wise leaders sidled up to Mambo. The gently nudged her with their trunks to confort her. Then the wise bull leader took a step back and trumpeted loudly. As the grove reverberated with his penetrating cry, Mambo shuddered next to the other cow. Finally, with a very gentle guttural sound the master bull began to speak.

He told Mambo of an elephant named Puspah. Puspah came from India, where she had served a royal family before being sent to America, where she was used for breeding. Now Puspah roams alone on the Makumbi Wildlife Preserve, where she is given special treatment because of her service and her age. Shani would be sent to Puspah. She has been known, from time to time, to pick up a young elephant and has been allowed to keep her young companions on the reserve. Puspah is very old. She will teach Shani wisdom gathered during her long life, the leader promises. Puspah has much to teach.

And so, a few weeks later, as the herd is on one of its noctural walks, Puspah appears and Shani follows her off to begin a new life.

On the Makumbi Wildlife Preserve, Shani immediately realizes that Puspah is very special. Not only is she different looking--her ears are smaller and she has no tusks--but she eats a special food. Peanuts, they're called, and they come from America. Puspah says they are a special treat for elephants in America.

After a few days it becomes apparent that Shani is addicted to the toasted, salty peanuts. Each day Puspah's supply disappears quickly---just as soon as they are set out for Puspah.

Finally, Puspah, seeing the young elephant's unintentional greediness, talks to Shani about this special snack. She tells him that she knows this tasty food grows in West Africa, and that he will have to find his own supply. After all, she likes her American treat and she has earned it with many years of service. She doesn't mind sharing, but Shani must not east her supply again.

Shani pushes away from Puspah and, for the next few days, spends much time alone. Finally, one hot, hot day as Shani lies in the cool water of a semi-shallow river bed, Puspah ambles down the bank to join him. Softly, she begins telling Shani of his abilities and his specialness.

"Becuase of your special talents, Shani you can give much to your fellow mammals and you can also find fulfillment for much of your inner restlessness."

Shani's ears spread wide to capture what the wise cow is saying.

"You mean I can find the toasted peanut tree here in Africa?"

"Did I say it was a tree? Well, yes, Shani, you can find toasted peanuts here in West Africa."

"But I don't know how, Puspah. I've looked, but I don't know what I'm really looking for and I don't know where to look and . . . "

"But, Shani, just to find these plants and eat them will only be a short-lived treat for you. What will you do when they're all gone? Think about this Shani. Wouldn't you like your Mother, Mambo, and others from your herd to taste them, too? How can you do this?"

"Well, first I have to find them and I don't know how to do that!"

"That is why I'm here, Shani. You will have to work, but I shall guide you."

An now, walk with baby elephant, Shani, as Puspah leads him on the research process and his independent study of the peanut in West Africa.

1. STATE THE PROBLEM OR QUESTION CORRECTLY IN WRITTEN FORM.

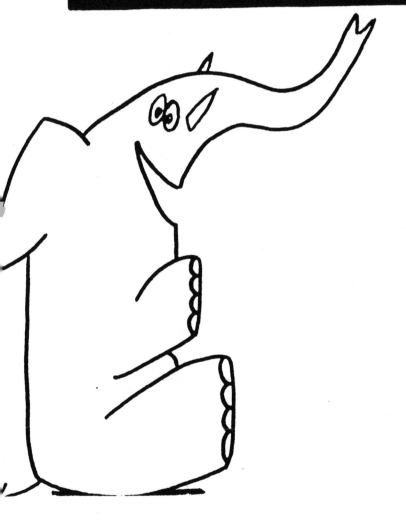

Do TOASTED peanuts really grow wild in West Africa? If so, where can they be found?

2. LIST THE BASIC INFORMATION ALREADY KNOWN.

Toasted peanuts taste good.

Toasted peanuts have crisp outer shells.

Toasted peanuts come in bags from America.

Toasted peanuts from America are often salty.

The shells must be cracked to get to the peanuts.

3. LIST OTHER QUESTIONS TO BE ANSWERED BEFORE YOU CAN ANSWER
    YOUR MAJOR QUESTION OR SOLVE YOUR MAJOR PROBLEM.

What does a toasted peanut plant look like?

How can toasted peanut plants be found?

Do toasted peanuts grow in patches, bushes, trees or underground?

Can you smell a peanut plant?

What are some uses for toasted peanuts besides snacks?

4. LIST SOURCES TO BE CONSULTED.

The West African Farmer's Almanac

Write to: American Peanut Farmers' Association
                 c/o Plains, Georgia
                 United States of America

Consult other African elephant herds.

Make an expedition to outlying areas.

Write to: Plants Nuts
                 c/o Mr. Peanut
                 New York City, New York 10022
                 United States of America

5. <u>LOCATE THOSE SOURCES.</u>

Reference Books

Card Catalog

Audiovisual materials

Nonfiction Books

Interviews

Field Trips

Public Library

Museums

Foreign Exporters

6. ACQUIRE SPECIFIC INFORMATION FROM THE SOURCES.

Use Table of Contents   Separate Fact from Opinion

Use the Index to a Book   Check Authorities

Use Encyclopedia Indexes   Check Facts in More than One Source

Use Skimming Skills   Get First Hand Accounts, If Possible

7. <u>TAKE NOTES.</u>

Peanuts grow on tops of trees where they are toasted by the hot African sun.

8. OUTLINE.

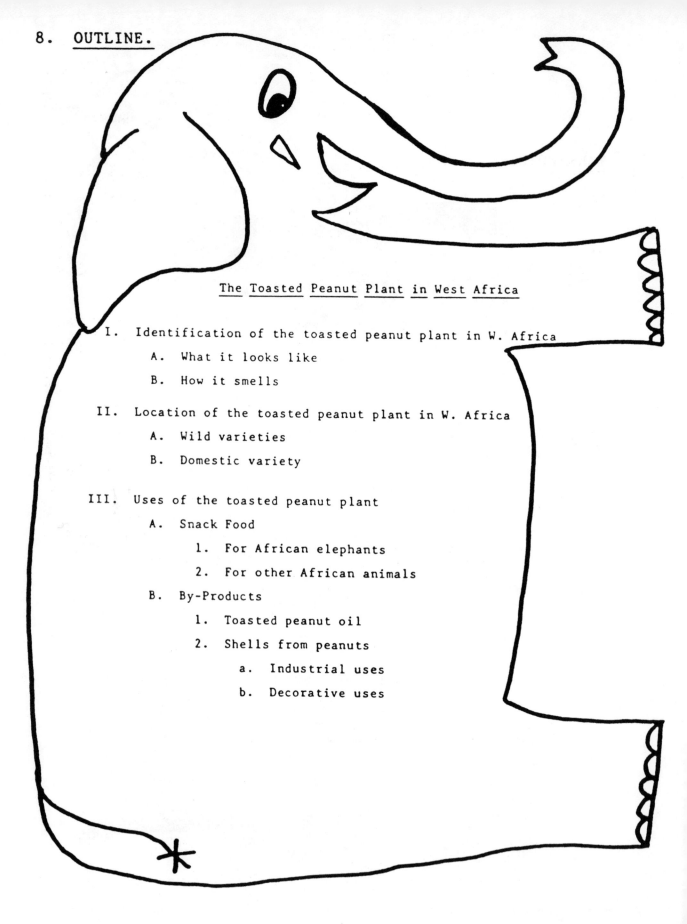

The Toasted Peanut Plant in West Africa

I.   Identification of the toasted peanut plant in W. Africa
    A.   What it looks like
    B.   How it smells

II.   Location of the toasted peanut plant in W. Africa
    A.   Wild varieties
    B.   Domestic variety

III.   Uses of the toasted peanut plant
    A.   Snack Food
        1.   For African elephants
        2.   For other African animals
    B.   By-Products
        1.   Toasted peanut oil
        2.   Shells from peanuts
            a.   Industrial uses
            b.   Decorative uses

9. PREPARE A FINISHED PRODUCT.

CONSIDER:

Report
Story
Poem
Letter
Newspaper
Graph
Chart
Diagram
Model
Tape
Filmstrip
Collection
Diary
Diorama
Map
Mobile
Questionnaire
Advertisement
Teach a Lesson
Cartoons
Play
Invention
Game
Bulletin Board

Debate
Comparison
Painting
Discussion
Composition
Simulation
Editorial
Letter
Recipe
Riddles
Journal

Others:

_____
_____
_____
_____

Add one barrel of rain water.

Heat under noon day Sun.

Serve.

Product of W. AFRICA

Ca...
TOAST
PEAN
SO...

10. SHARE THE PRODUCT.

IDEAS FOR PRODUCTS

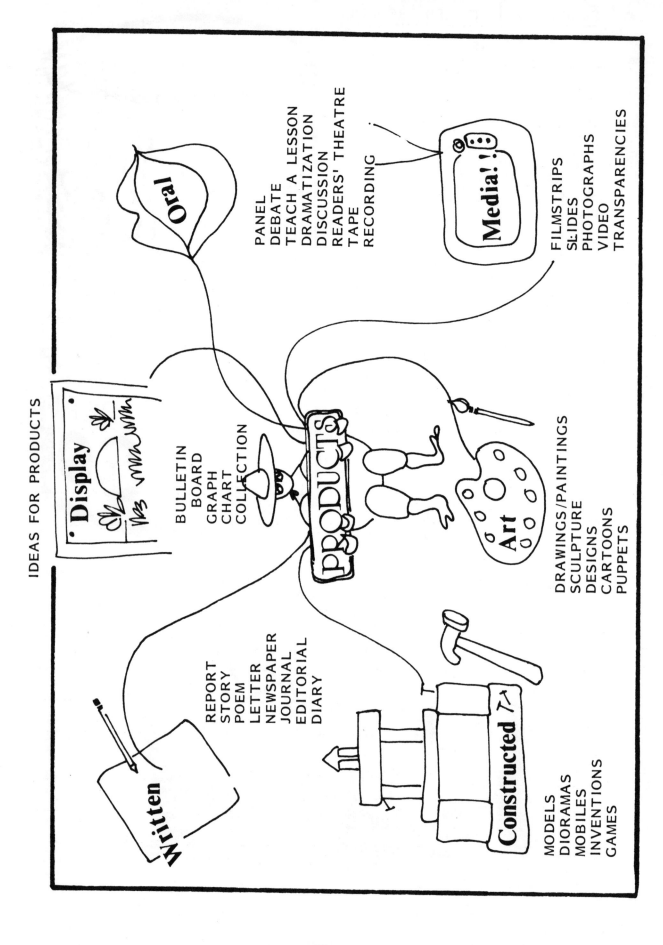

Oral

PANEL
DEBATE
TEACH A LESSON
DRAMATIZATION
DISCUSSION
READERS' THEATRE
TAPE
RECORDING

Media!!

FILMSTRIPS
SLIDES
PHOTOGRAPHS
VIDEO
TRANSPARENCIES

Display

BULLETIN
BOARD
GRAPH
CHART
COLLECTION

PRODUCTS

Art

DRAWINGS/PAINTINGS
SCULPTURE
DESIGNS
CARTOONS
PUPPETS

Written

REPORT
STORY
POEM
LETTER
NEWSPAPER
JOURNAL
EDITORIAL
DIARY

Constructed

MODELS
DIORAMAS
MOBILES
INVENTIONS
GAMES

Name _____

NOTETAKING

SOURCE _____

_____

PAGES _____

INFORMATION SOUGHT _____

_____

_____

WHAT THIS SOURCE SAYS _____

_____

_____

_____

_____

_____

IMPORTANT QUOTATIONS _____

_____

PAGE NUMBER OF QUOTE _____

_____

_____

PAGE NUMBER OF QUOTE _____

INFORMATION STILL NEEDED _____

_____

_____

Name _____

BIBLIOGRAPHIES

ENCYCLOPEDIA

1. _____

   _____

2. _____

   _____

BOOKS

1. _____

   _____

2. _____

   _____

3. _____

   _____

PERIODICALS (Author listed)

1. _____

   _____

2. _____

   _____

3. _____

   _____

PERIODICALS (No author listed)

1. _____

   _____

2. _____

   _____

Name _____

OUTLINING

I. _____

    A. _____

    B. _____

    C. _____

        1. _____

        2. _____

II. _____

    A. _____

    B. _____

III. _____

    A. _____

        1. _____

        2. _____

        3. _____

    B. _____

        1. _____

        2. _____

        3. _____

        4. _____

    C. _____

INTERVIEWING

Name _____

TOPIC _____

PERSON INTERVIEWED _____
                   (Name, in full, and title, if one)

QUESTION #1 _____
            _____

ANSWER _____
       _____

QUESTION #2 _____
            _____

ANSWER _____
       _____

QUESTION #3 _____
            _____

ANSWER _____
       _____

QUESTION #4 _____
            _____

ANSWER _____
       _____

QUESTION #5 _____
            _____

ANSWER _____
       _____

SUMMARY OF THIS INTERVIEW _____
                          _____
                          _____

INFORMATION STILL NEEDED _____
                         _____

SUMMARY SHEET

Name _____   Date _____

Teacher _____   Grade _____

TOPIC
Describe the problem you will investigate.   What are you going to investigate?   What do you hope to find out?

_____

_____

_____

_____

PRODUCT
Describe the product you hope to produce.

_____

_____

METHODS and MATERIALS
Describe the types of information or data that you will need to solve this problem.   Where will you begin looking for this information?   List some of the sources you plan to consult.

_____

_____

_____

_____

_____

_____

_____

_____

PROGRESS   REPORTS

First progress date   _____

Second progress date   _____

Third progress date   _____

NOTES FROM YOUR TEACHERS
On the other side of this sheet you will find some notes, helps, and suggestions from your teacher about your project.   Be sure to keep this sheet and write down any questions or ideas you want to discuss with your teacher on the next progress date.

PROJECT   COMPLETION
On the line below give the date that you think you will probably be finished with your project. This could change as you begin doing research and working on your plans, but try to set a tentative date for the completion of your project.

_____

EVALUATION

1) Determine criteria

2) Determine rating scale

3) Evaluate

A.	Topic or problem Selection	–	simple	1	2	3	4	5	challenging
B.	Development of hypothesis	–	trivial	1	2	3	4	5	complex
C.	Development of questions	–	lower order	1	2	3	4	5	higher order
D.	Use of resources	–	few	1	2	3	4	5	many
E.	Research	–	deficient	1	2	3	4	5	extensive
F.	Product	–	poorly developed	1	2	3	4	5	well developed
G.	Communication of study to others	–	ineffective	1	2	3	4	5	effective
H.	Overall rating	–	inadequate	1	2	3	4	5	well done

Additional comments:

_____

_____

_____

_____

_____

_____

_____

_____

_____

Bendick, Jeanne   <u>AUTOMOBILES</u>   Franklin Watts

A. There are many different kinds of automobiles discussed in this book. Which one would you like to own? Write a paragraph describing that car and one telling what you would be thinking and feeling when you first got in your car, as well as where you would go. Who would go with you?

B. Write about one of the engines this book shows. How does it work? What might be advantages to using this engine? What might be some disadvantages?

C. There are several problems that have been mentioned in this book. Pick one of these problems and draw a cartoon to illustrate it. Then write your ideas on how the problem might be solved on another sheet of paper.

Coffman, Ramon P. and   <u>FAMOUS EXPLORERS</u> <u>FOR</u> <u>YOUNG</u>
Goodman, Nathan G.   <u>PEOPLE</u>

                                        Dodd, Mead & Co

A. Pick one of these explorers and write about their journeys or discoveries. Illustrate your story with a drawing, chart, or time line.

B. Choose two of these explorers. Write about a particular danger each one faced. Then write another paragraph explaining which explorer faced the greatest danger, in your opinion.

C. Make a chart showing each explorer, what they discovered and when, what country they were from, and when they lived.

D. If you could have gone along on one of these trips, which would you pick? Why? Write about your answers.

RESEARCH CARDS 4-6

Eberle, Irmengarde   FAMOUS INVENTORS FOR YOUNG PEOPLE

Dodd, Mead & Co

A. Choose one person from this book and write about how that person became famous.
B. Make your own invention, illustrate it and write about it. What made you think of it? Is it something that someone might need? What materials would you use to make it?
C. Choose some invention not shown in this book and write a short report about how it was invented and by whom.
D. Pick one of these inventions and trace how it has changed over the years. Has it been improved? Was anything else discovered because of this discovery or invention?

Fisher, Leonard Everett   TWO IF BY SEA Random House

A. This book tells about an important night in our nation's history. Make a picture story that shows one of the things that happened on this night.
B. Choose one of the characters in this story. Write a poem that tells about his part in history.
C. Pretend you are one of these famous men. How might you have felt about each problem that you faced that night. How would you have felt as you took action against the British?
D. Often these people found themselves having to wait for something or someone. How might these people have felt? List all the descriptive words and phrases you can think of to describe that feeling. Write a story in which you make up a situation and use as many of your words and phrases as possible to show how your character feels as he or she waits for something very important to happen.

RESEARCH CARDS 4-6

Gross, Ruth Belov   MONEY, MONEY, MONEY

                                      Four Winds Press

A. What does barter mean? Was it always a good thing to
   use? Why or why not? Write your answers to these
   questions and give examples to support your opinions.
B. What are some of the things that used to be used as
   money? Illustrate four or five different kinds of money
   and write a short description underneath each one.
C. If you were king of a new country, what kind of system
   would you use: barter or money? What would you decide
   was valuable in your country? What would you use for
   money if you needed it? Write your answers, give reasons
   for your decisions, and illustrate the system you decide
   upon.

Henry, Marguerite   ALBUM OF HORSES   Rand McNally

A. Write a description of the physical appearance and the
   general temperament of three of these horses.
B. Choose one animal in this book. Write about and illustrate
   what you find out about it in this book.
C. Choose one of these animals. Pretend that you are one of
   this breed. Write a story about the most exciting day of
   your life.

RESEARCH CARDS

4-6

Ingraham, Leonard W.   AN ALBUM OF COLONIAL AMERICA

Franklin Watts

A. Pick one area of colonial life. Tell briefly what it was like then, and then tell how you think it is now. Compare them. Which way would you rather live? Write your reasons explaining your response.
B. Pick one of the colonial heroes and write a story of his or her life.
C. Write a story about something that could have happened in colonial times. This should be realistic fiction.
D. Write a stort explanation of the events and reasons leading to the Revolutionary War.

Lyon, Nancy   MYSTERY OF STONEHENGE

Raintree Childrens Books

A. There are many stories about how and why Stonehenge was formed. Make up your own story about Stonehenge's origin and illustrate it.
B. Make a fact chart listing all of the facts known about Stonehenge. Make small illustrations occasionally to make your chart more interesting.
C. Chapter Five discusses the physical layout of Stonehenge. Draw a map of what Stonehenge might have looked like using this information. Label the various areas.
D. Chapter Six discusses bluestones. Where did they come from? How could the Beaker People transport them? Do you agree with the book about how it was done? Write an explanation of your opinion and give your reasons for supporting or disagreeing with the book.

Mussbaum, Hedda   PLANTS DO AMAZING THINGS

Random House

A. Imagine a new plant that can do something almost
   unbelievable! Write about this plant, what it looks like,
   and its unusual abilities. Illustrate your description.
B. Choose one of these unusual plants. Write a story about
   it using pictures and very short captions. In this story
   show what you have learned about this plant.
C. If you could bring two of these plants to school, which
   ones would you bring? Why? Write about your choices and
   the reasons you picked them. Which one is your favorite?

Pettit, Ted S.   THE WEB OF NATURE

Doubleday

A. Choose one relationship between living things and explain
   it in your own words. Illustrate this relationship.
B. What is a natural community? Pick one of the communities
   discussed here and write a description of its
   characteristics. Write about how it came to be that way.
   What are some of the living things you would expect to
   find there?
C. Man can have a great influence on his environment. Write
   about how some people are trying to keep the web of
   nature intact and balanced.

Pringle, Laurence   THE ONLY EARTH WE HAVE

Macmillan Co.

A. Make a poster to show how nature recycles things and how living things depend on each other to survive.
B. Draw a cartoon in which you show some ways in which man is harming the environment. Then draw another cartoon in which you show one way that man could help the environment.
C. Write some suggestions about ways we can keep our "spaceship" Earth in balance and working smoothly.

Ronan, Margaret   ALL ABOUT OUR FIFTY STATES

Random House

A. Pick a state that you might like to live in or visit. Gather as much information as you can find. Make a travel guide for the class to see. Include a map and several places they might like to see.
B. Make a chart showing the states, their capitals, state flowers, state flags, state birds, and the year each became a state. Illustrate your chart.
C. Draw a map of one state. On this map, write some of the things the state produces, its population in 1962 (from this book), and the most recent population count you can find.

RESEARCH CARDS 4-6

Smith, Howard E., Jr.   ANIMAL OLYMPICS

Doubleday

A. Choose ten events from this book. Make a chart showing which animal would win each event, and the reason it would win. Illustrate your chart.
B. Find out and write a report about one of the animals that you did not know much about. Some suggestions: chamois, ibex, klipspringer, voles, yak.
C. Make a new event for the Animal Olympics. Write a description of the event. Which animals could enter this event? Which one do you think would win? Give reasons to support your answer.

Zim, Herbert S.   SHARKS   Wm. Morrow & Co.

A. Choose one type of shark. Write a report about it. Arrange to present this report to your reading group or to the class.
B. Make a shark safety poster. Show what attracts sharks, how they attack and the best preventive measures discussed in this book.
C. Make a list of the physical characteristics of sharks. Then make up a "new" species of shark. Write a description of this new species and make an illustration.

RESEARCH CARDS

4-6

CHOOSE A FOLKTALE. USE IT TO
COMPLETE THE CHARTS BELOW.

NAME _____

Culture Comparison Charts

TITLE OF FOLKTALE_____

Elements of Culture		Title of Tale	Your Culture
Most popular means of transportation			
Most popular medium for information			
Most popular music			
Most respected profession (s)			
Role of male	Active? Passive?		
Role of female	Involved? Onlooker? Assertive? Submissive?		

This tale is set in _____century _____.

country

Differing Philosophies/Beliefs		
VALUE	Folktale Culture	Our Culture
Life Goals		
Treatment of Nature		
Material Possessions		
Work Ethic		
Family Life		
Use of Time		

Research Project:

Produce a mini-newspaper based on a book of fiction.

Objectives:

To become acquainted with the parts of a newspaper; to interpret a book of fiction in original ways; to use specific research skills in a functional situation.

Materials Needed

1. Favorite book of fiction
2. Six newspaper research cards
3. Selected research sources.

Procedure:

Read the information and follow directions and examples on the research cards to produce your own newspaper. Follow this structure of feature articles:

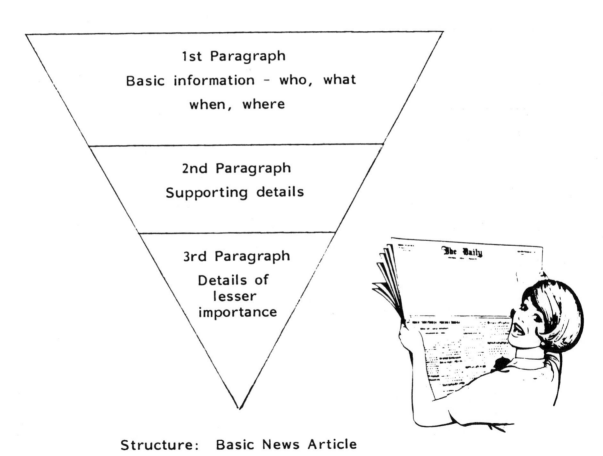

Structure: Basic News Article

NEWSPAPER   CARD 1

FRONT PAGE

The front page is the most important part of the newspaper. It contains the BIG story of the day. The next few important stories also go on page one.

NEWSPAPER   CARD

FINANCIAL PAGE

This page contains news on new businesses and products. It also contains news about the economy.

NEWSPAPER   CARD 2

EDITORIAL PAGE

Only on this page is the writer or editor allowed to voice his own feelings and opinions about a subject. Editorial or political cartoons which voice an opinion are also included.

NEWSPAPER   CARD 5

FEATURE SECTION

This section of the paper contains a variety of information for and about people. Here are a few of the things you would find in the feature section:

- Fashion News   Advice or
- Book & Movie   Personal
   Reviews   Columns
- TV, Radio, Movie Puzzles
   Schedules   Homemaking
- Restaurants   Hints
- Comic Strips   Humor

NEWSPAPER   CARD 3

SPORTS PAGE

The sports page keeps readers up-to-date on sports around the area and the country. Charts of scores and photos are also included.

NEWSPAPER   CARD 6

ADVERTISING

This section contains information in the form of ads for jobs, cars, homes, new and used products, etc.

FINANCIAL PAGE   ACTIVITY 4

Use the setting of the book to examine the money angle of the story.

Mary Poppins
Current pay for domestic workers
Cost to homeowners for chimney sweep service
Current airline fares to South Pole from London
Research – wages for various occupations. Airline rates and projected increases.

FEATURE SECTION   ACTIVITY 5

From Mary Poppins
Comic strip about Mary and children
London fashions
A Dear Mary column
Crossword puzzle
Word search
Believe It or Not column

Research: Other items found in the feature section of your local paper.

ADVERTISING   ACTIVITY 6

Design new products or run want ads for characters from your book.

From Mary Poppins

Fly   No
with   more
your very   waiting
own   for
umbrella   airplanes!

Research classified ads.

FRONT PAGE   ACTIVITY 1

Here is where the plot of the book is revealed. Think of major headlines and follow with short news stories describing the action.

STRANGE RAIN!

Children Kidnapped by Maid

Research: weather phenomena and laws pertaining to kidnapping.
short news stories decribing the action.

EDITORIAL PAGE   ACTIVITY 2

Do you have an opinion about some part of the story. Speak up!

Households should or should not be ruled by fathers.
Pay too low for child care workers
Education level higher outside school than IN school

Research on current information levels, current pay for child care workers.

SPORTS PAGE   ACTIVITY 3

Find sports-related topics for articles. Be creative.

Chimney-Sweep Olympics
Ends in Tie

More People Try Flying
As a Hobby

Research on sports popular in England in 1900.

SEARCHING THE NEWSPAPER!

ANIMALS IN THE NEWS

Using magazines and newspapers, find pictures and/or headlines which are examples for the following items:

1. A mammal of your state.

2. What an insect might eat.

3. An animal you'd like for a pet.

4. Something a squirrel might use in his nest.

5. Someone's opinion of hunting.

6. A reason for damming a stream.

7. Where an insect might live.

8. A wild animal you might find in your home.

9. Something that would pollute a stream.

10. An example of what happens when you use insecticides.

11. An animal who does not need legs to move.

12. An industry that might pollute.

13. An animal that requires magnification to be seen.

14. A way in which you might help an animal live.

15. An animal that lives underground.

16. The name of someone to write to about an environmental concern.

17. The usual number of mice in a litter.

18. An animal you might find on a decaying log.

19. Something a robin might eat.

20. A reptile of your state.

The Newspaper and Productive Thinking

Fluency: The ability to make many responses.

    a. Name as many kinds of foods as you can which might appear in a grocery ad in the newspaper. Check one ad to see items you missed.

    b. Make a list of things which might be advertised for sale under FURNITURE in the want ads. Check one day's want ads to see items you missed.

    c. List as many comic characters as you can. Look in your local paper and check those who appear.

Flexibility: The ability to define categories

    a. How many different types of things might be for sale in the want ads?

    b. Cut different stories from the paper. Categorize the stories under major headlines.

    c. How many types of comic strips are there in your paper? What major categories do they fall under?

Elaboration:

    a. Add one additional paragraph to a news story of your choice.

    b. Draw three more frames to complete a comic strip.

    c. Select a headline and change it to give it a different meaning.

Originality:

    a. Read one lonely hearts letter without reading the solution. Write your own solution to the problem.

    b. Using the reporter's format, write a news story of an actual event that has taken place in your school.

    c. Write an original editorial on the topic: Proposal for a Four Day School Week.

Critical Thinking Skills

Planning: Plan a well-balanced meal using one page of food ads.

Forecasting: Read an Ann Landers problem. Predict what her reply will be.

Decision Making: You have $50.00 to spend. Select from the ads a complete new outfit.

Problem Solving: Select one front page story. Define the basic problem. List as many solutions as you can to the problem. Establish criteria for selecting the best solution. Choose one.

Evaluation: Read the movie reviews for one day. Select one film you would like to see. List reasons for your choice. Select one film you would not want to see. List reasons for rejecting the film.

PROPAGANDA TECHNIQUES

Analyzing methods used by propagandists in advertisements.

1. Analogy: This car is a one owner car so it has to be better than any other used car you could buy.
2. Superstition: During the downtown renewal project you don't have to walk under any ladders to find the bargains in our store.
3. Faulty Arguments: Buy now while interest rates are low.
4. Generalizations: Everyone is hurrying to XYZ car dealers to get in on the bargains.
5. Appeal to Ignorance: Tried other Doctors? Now try Doctor X. I can cure heart trouble, cancer, headaches, and nervous conditions through adjustment of the spine which controls all body functions.
6. Ego Trip: It costs a little more, but YOU'RE worth it.
7. Argument in a Circle: Our computer dating service has matched hundreds of happy couples, many of whom are now happily married, so you, too, should join now.
8. Emotional Appeal: Prowlers are on the loose in our town. Keep YOUR family safe, call ABC burglar alarms today.
9. Faulty Use of Statistics: Mary B. lost 30 pounds in 24 days. Our weight loss graduates lose more weight than in any other program.
10. Vagueness: Everyone is talking about the new Edsel!
11. Choice of Words: Super, great, best ever, wild sale, astonishing new product. It's a Communist plot.
12. Repetition: (Slogans) Reach out, reach out and touch someone. (Bell Telephone)
13. Exaggeration: Related to choice of language. Come in today, don't miss the Sale of a Lifetime!
14. Quoting Out of Context: From a book review: "Not worth reading, the bigger than life characters have appeal only when well handled by a competent author...this author certainly is not competent." Pattonville Times. Book ad says: PATTONVILLE TIMES REVIEWER SAYS "BIGGER THAN LIFE CHARACTERS HAVE APPEAL..."
15. Half Truths: "She was treated in a mental hospital." The "she" in question was injured in an automobile accident and taken to the nearest emergency room which happened to be in a hospital most noted for its treatment of mental patients.
16. Omitting Pertinent Facts: In a recent nuclear power accident the news media was instructed to omit facts which would have indicated the true extent of the danger of nearby residents.
17. The Bandwagon Approach: Don't miss this big event, EVERYONE will be there.
18. "Just Like One of the Boys": Vote for Mr. X. He's born and raised in this town and knows the folks and their problems.
19. Transfer: Long distance is the next best thing to being there.
20. Snob Appeal: For those who want the very best! or Where the great meet to eat.
21. Name Dropping or Name Calling: Miss Blank (a famous movie star) used this brand.
22. Testimonials: Hospital tested! Recommended by more doctors than any other brand.

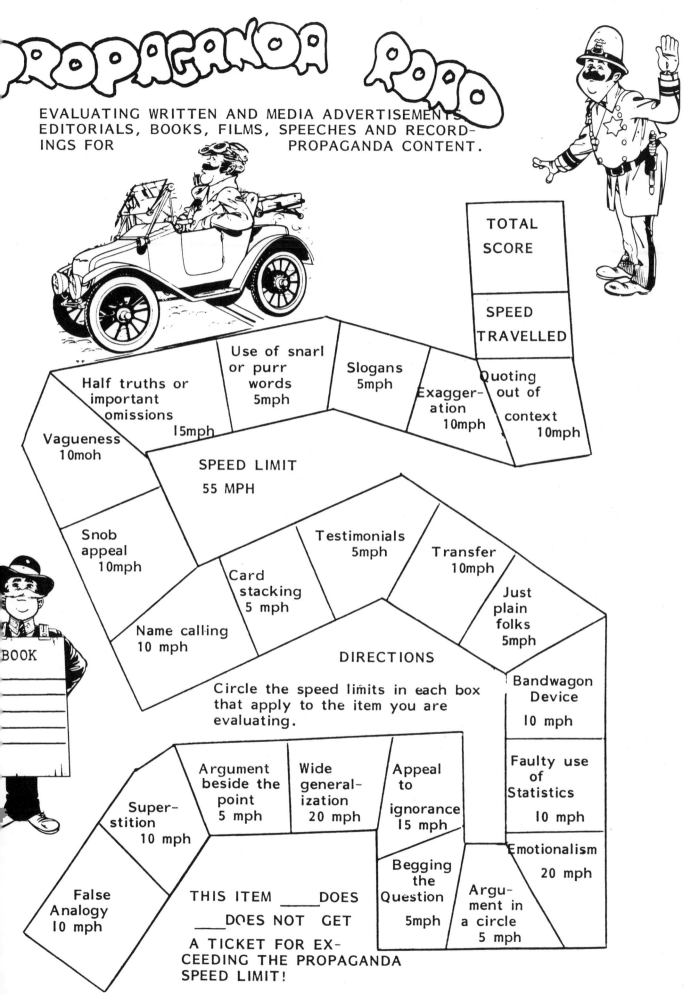

PROPAGANDA ROAD

EVALUATING WRITTEN AND MEDIA ADVERTISEMENTS, EDITORIALS, BOOKS, FILMS, SPEECHES AND RECORDINGS FOR PROPAGANDA CONTENT.

TOTAL SCORE

SPEED TRAVELLED

Half truths or important omissions 15mph

Use of snarl or purr words 5mph

Slogans 5mph

Exaggeration 10mph

Quoting out of context 10mph

Vagueness 10moh

SPEED LIMIT 55 MPH

Snob appeal 10mph

Testimonials 5mph

Transfer 10mph

Card stacking 5 mph

Name calling 10 mph

Just plain folks 5mph

DIRECTIONS

Circle the speed limits in each box that apply to the item you are evaluating.

Bandwagon Device 10 mph

BOOK

Super-stition 10 mph

Argument beside the point 5 mph

Wide general-ization 20 mph

Appeal to ignorance 15 mph

Faulty use of Statistics 10 mph

Emotionalism 20 mph

False Analogy 10 mph

THIS ITEM ____ DOES ____ DOES NOT GET A TICKET FOR EXCEEDING THE PROPAGANDA SPEED LIMIT!

Begging the Question 5mph

Argument in a circle 5 mph

In this section you will explore the lives of people who were/are gifted in many different fields of endeavor. Unfortunately, the giftedness of many of these people was not recognized in their lifetimes.

The story below and the BIOGRAPHY IN BLOOM activities which follow provide a good model for the examination of the lives of other gifted persons.

In reading the story and completing the activities you are to determine whether CATNIP BILL is or is not a gifted person.

CATNIP BILL (THE HOBO)
by Pete Smith Ⓒ 1978

It was sometime in early Spring each year and perhaps on an evening just after dusk where we might sense that Catnip Bill had returned once again for a visit to our neck of the woods. Now Bill wasn't a readin' man, don't know that he could, but he knew more about the outdoors than any scientist with a PhD. He acquired the name Catnip Bill from the children around there, there along the northern shores of Massachusetts, around Cape Ann, because at a certain time of the year they'd spot him roaming the hills in search of wild herbs. You see Bill was a wild weed expert; he knew all about the wonders of the healing powers many of them contained, many of which were only spices and elixirs but he also picked the wild Catnip.

Now, one might get the idea that Bill was back in our neck of the woods for his yearly pilgrimage on a night with all of the windows to our house opened wide to let in the fresh smell of Pine trees and Lilac blossom, when we would suddenly be overtaken by the sweet smell of his pipe tobacco. We would rush to the window sills and lean out only to see his fading shadow in the dark and hear the sounds of his shuffling feet off in the distance. He would pass by with that lingering aroma of Kenick-kenick smoke trailing behind from that old pipe. Kenick-kenick is another one of those weeds that grew on the hillsides and he'd pick it and mix it with his pouch tobacco while on his search for the Wild Catnip. Catnip is an herb that was sometimes used for healing but was most commonly used to excite and rearrange a kittycat's behavior; given in small amounts just to make them act silly; this of course amused children. Bill's bag should of read, "Smiles for sale!"

Sometimes he appeared in the daylight up in the hills, bent over, carrying his brown paper shopping bag that contained everything he owned. He didn't need much. He was a free soul and he seemed contented with his sparse ways. He loved folks, for sure..could talk on any subject and when he spoke in that wise old voice of his there was something that just compelled a body to stop and listen.

He was somewhat of a raggedy old soul with a big beard and was always clothed for winter time wearing his long wool coat and worn out hat.

If we were lucky enough to have a daytime encounter with him, I say lucky for you see we might not have another chance to see Bill until later in the summer, but on that lucky day when we caught up with him he'd tell us about wild things; things that were free.While he talked he'd pick up some small piece of wood and carve little animal creatures from them and give these tiny treasures of art to us.

We'd follow him down from the hills and walk with him as we passed houses, occasionally stopping to knock someone's door. The door would open and he'd say "You got any kitty cats? Because I've got some catnip here for fifteen cents a bunch!" in his old aging high pitched creeky voice. And most everyone did buy some.

And of course if you missed him, you knew he'd passed on through shortly before because there were kitties drapped and groggy in the trees, barely hanging by a thread, with big grins on their faces lying back swatting with a huge lack of sincerity at some passing butterfly or bumble bee; acting careless over strange dogs passing by!

I know he traveled with the weather because we last saw him each year just as Fall showed its first signs. He would do some more gathering and preparing for his travels to other places.

Some suggested that the train trestle and tracks that led into the city and the station played a role in his appearance and disappearance each year.

They said that he probably traveled south when it got cold and all the leaves began turning and falling and there would be the last sounds of leaves shuffling with two feet whispering on down the road.

A Study of Biography: The Gifted and Talented

1. KNOWLEDGE/COMPREHENSION:Objective: Students will be able to distinguish character traits associated with the gifted and talented.

    A. (Productive thinking, fluency) List many indications of giftedness or talent which were displayed by the character.
    B. Find specific words or phrases used to describe his talent or ability.

2. APPLICATION: Objective: The student will evaluate common beliefs about gifted persons.

    A. Using your character which statements can you prove to be true or false?

        1. Talent in one area means weakness in another.
        2. Ability in early years wears out.
        3. Gifted persons are more likely to become emotionally disturbed.
        4. Gifted children always do well in school.
        5. Gifted people are hard to understand.
        6. Gifted people do not enjoy life.
        7. Gifted people are physically weak and sickly.

3. ANALYSIS: Objective: The student will realize that giftedness is a condition determined in part by the culture in which a person lives.

    A. What aspects of the character's giftedness might have been valued in a frontier culture (early American frontier for example)?
    B. What aspects are valued in our culture?
    C. The town deputy has put this character in jail for vagrancy.
    Plan a defense?
    MATERIALS NEEDED: Authorities you would consult, evidence you would gather
    STEPS: How would you present the case? What would you bring up first, second, etc.? When would you call certain witnesses?
    PROBLEMS: List problems you might have. This could include negative aspects that others might bring out. Tell how you would combat each problem.

4. SYNTHESIS: Objective: Using the details of the character the student will predict the character's behavior in a new setting.

    A. Dramatize with impromptu dialogue:
        1. He has been wrongly jailed for assault.
        2. He is visiting with our first interplanetary visitor.
        3. He has been elected leader of the country.
        4. He has just become a parent.

5. EVALUATION: Objective: The student will decide which traits of gifted are valued by our society today and discuss ways in which interpersonal friction can be minimized.

    A. In your group, outline a "what if" story. This character has come to live permanently in your community. Which of his talents would be valued? Would he be considered gifted? Which traits of character would be apt to cause difficulty for him? How could we help him resolve this problem?

BIOGRAPHY IN BLOOM

images of greatness

by David Melton

IMAGES OF GREATNESS serves as a gentle reminder of how the achievements and the contributions of many gifted people have enriched our heritage, influenced our lives today and will enhance the future of the world.

1. Identify the area of contribution to society of each of the following:

2. TAKE A MESSAGE! Choose two people below. One has called and left a message for the other. What was the message?

Pablo Casals	Ted Geisel	Charles Dickens
Katherine Hepburn	Winston Churchill	Thornton Wilder
Benjamin Spock	Arturo Toscanini	Bob Hope
Eleanor Roosevelt	Golda Meir	Margaret Chase Smith
Marie Curie	Booker T. Washington	Albert Schweitzer
Pearl Bailey	Bing Crosby	Douglas MacArthur
Sir Charles Chaplin	Igor Stravinsky	Helen Keller
Norman Rockwell	Pearl S. Buck	Arthur Fiedler
Margaret Mead	Norman Vincent Peale	Robert Browning
Casey Stengel	Lillian Carter	Marc Chagall
Thomas Edison	Linus Pauling	Jimmy Durante
Walt Whitman	Mary Baker Eddy	Martha Graham
Kate Smith	Leroy Paige	Dwight Eisenhower
Grandma Moses	Jesse Owens	Samuel Goldwyn

Brainstorm with your class or a group and list all of the statements about gifted people that you believe to be true. Select one of the gifted persons listed above. Locate at least three separate sources of information about the person. How many of the statements you have listed apply to this particular gifted person's life?

1. Ex: Those who show giftedness at an early age burn out later. _____

2. _____

3. _____

4. _____

5. _____

IMAGES OF GREATNESS is a beautifully illustrated book of quotations of the famous. Compiled and illustrated by David Melton. Independence Press.

BIOGRAPHY INVENTORS

Below are the names of ten well known inventors. After each name identify one major invention of each.

Benjamin Franklin _____   John Deere _____

Robert Fulton _____   Elisha Otis _____

Eli Whitney _____   Alexander G. Bell _____

Thomas A. Edison _____   John W. Hyatt _____

Elias Howe _____   Samuel F.B. Morse _____

Researching Inventors!

1. Read about the many inventions of Benjamin Franklin. List his inventions and cite those, if any, which are still in use today.

2. You are a southern farmer in 1753. Write a letter to Mr. Whitney expressing your feelings about his invention.

3. Set up an evaluation T listing the desirable and undesirable aspects of Alexander Graham Bell's most famous invention.

4. Inventions are often improved upon as time passes. Select one of the inventions listed above and predict ways in which it will be improved in the year 2020.

5. Suppose Elias Otis had left doors out of his invention. Think of ways the invention could still be used.

6. Once a light bulb burns out it is usually thrown away. How many uses can you think of for a burned out bulb?

7. Which of the inventions above have led to the development of other inventions. What were these other inventions?

8. Unless an emergency arises, go for three days without a telephone. Before beginning the experiment predict the effects this will have on your life. Which predictions were true? What effects were not predicted?

9. How many objects can you name would not exist today if it were not for John Hyatt's invention?

10. Predict how a seamstress in 1846 might have reacted to Mr. Howe's invention. Would the reaction have been universally favorable? If not, why not?

The Annual Arts Award

Select one of the years listed below.

1650   1700   1750   1800   1850   1900

Research the major creative persons alive and working during the year you choose. Which person during that particular year would be most likely to receive an award for his or her accomplishments? What group or organization would give the award (must be an actual group in existence at that time)? For what is the award given? Be specific.

Artists   **Actors/ ♫ Musicians**   **Authors**

_____   _____   _____

_____   _____   _____

_____

This award is presented to _____

by _____

Design the Award

PHOTO PUZZLERS!!

If you can answer these questions you are an A-1 Researcher!

This statue and others like it can be found in Aspen, Colorado. What is it made of? Can you find information about the maker?

This sign appears on the bridge over the Royal Gorge. WHY would no fishing be allowed?

The early Indians were flexible thinkers! How many different uses did they have for this plant.

The name of the plant is the BROADLEAF YUCCA.

Can you find at least twelve uses? More ??

A) This large tree stump is found on the battlefield at Shiloh. It commemorates the death from battle wounds of what famous Confederate General?

B) The glacier in the photograph below appears to be white in color. Glaciers, however are not white. What color are glaciers? What is the reason for this unusual color?

C) Find unusual photos in magazines. Develop a photo puzzler page for others to solve!

RESEARCH ACTIVITIES 7-8

CONTENTS

1. The Research Process: Contract and/or Guidelines
2. Mini-Projects-Research Cards
3. Comparison Research
4. Researching Car Ownership
5. Learning Styles
6. Leadership:Analyzing and Comparing Famous Leaders
7. The Gifted and Moral Development
8. Crossroads! Important Decisions in the Lives of the Great
9. Researching Historical Decisions
10. Researching Power!
11. Field Investigation: The Cemetery
12. Producing A Local History Reference Book

GOALS

SELF-SELECTED TOPICS, PROCESS, MATERIALS, RESOURCES, PRODUCTS

SELF-DIRECTED LEARNING

RESEARCH BEYOND THE WALLS OF THE SCHOOL

CREATIVE APPROACHES TO PRODUCTS

SELF EVALUATION

MAKING THE GOAL IN RESEARCH

Basic research skills enable one to locate information quickly and easily for ANY purpose. Knowing the process can speed up the search!

STEP ONE: Isolate the major topic or problem to be investigated.

Examples: Sources of teen income
Cost of car ownership
Rock Stars: Separating
Fact from Fiction
Football heroes

MAJOR TOPIC or PROBLEM

STEP TWO: Define the topic or problem by asking the right questions. Use the journalist's time-honored method!

A. WHO _____

B. WHAT _____

C. WHEN _____

D. WHERE _____

E. WHY _____

F. HOW _____

G. WHAT IF OR SUPPOSE THAT _____

H. OPINIONS _____

I. CONCLUSIONS _____

J. IMAGINATION _____

STEP THREE: WHERE TO LOOK (SOURCES)

Interviews _____   Encyclopedia _____

Card Catalog _____   Reference Books _____

Magazine(s) _____   Officials _____

_____   Organizations _____

Almanac _____   Other _____

DETERMINE A PROCESS

_____ Discover	_____ Compare	_____ Simulate	_____ Contrast
_____ Identify	_____ Construct	_____ Report	_____ Survey
_____ Locate	_____ Paint	_____ Experiment	_____ Editoralize
_____ List	_____ Interview	_____ Classify	_____ Recommend
_____ Debate	_____ Discuss	_____ Write	_____ Produce
_____ Invent	_____ Compose	_____ Match	_____ Record
_____ Other _____			

DETERMINE A PRODUCT

_____ Report	_____ Chart	_____ Diorama	_____ Play
_____ Story	_____ Diagram	_____ Map	_____ Invention
_____ Poem	_____ Model	_____ Mobile	_____ Game
_____ Letter	_____ Tape	_____ Questionnaire	_____ Bulletin Board
_____ Panel	_____ Filmstrip	_____ Advertisement	_____ Other
_____ Newspaper	_____ Collection	_____ Teach a lesson	_____
_____ Graph	_____ Diary	_____ Cartoons	_____

Summary:

Topic

Research Sources (Major)

Basic Processes

Expected Product

Time Limit

ASKING GOOD QUESTIONS!

Questions for research can be unusual, stimulating and mind-stretching or trivial, easy and boring.

Here are two questions on the human brain. Which would be more interesting to research?

1. What are the parts of the human brain? (Knowledge question)

2. If the left brain dominant person (logical mind) wanted to become more right brain dominant (creative mind) what would he or she need to do? Is this possible? (Analysis question).

THINK ABOUT THE KINDS OF QUESTIONS YOU WANT TO ASK:

QUESTIONS TO THINK ABOUT!

Select a topic. Develop questions on this topic using the questioning model below.

QUANTITY QUESTION

How many ways might _____?

REORGANIZATION QUESTION

What would have happened if or what would happen if _____

_____?

SUPPOSITION QUESTION

How would _____ change or be different if _____

_____?

VIEWPOINT QUESTION

How would _____ look to or be interpreted by

_____(person's name)?

INVOLVEMENT QUESTION

If you _____

what would you say or do?

FORCED ASSOCIATION QUESTION

How is _____ like _____?

This type of question seeks common elements between two seemingly unrelated events or persons.

EVALUATION QUESTION

What is or was the ultimate value of _____?

Each of the above questions should require the development of additional questions to be answered as supporting data.

ALCOHOLISM

1. What causes this disease?
2. Are some people more likely to become alcoholics?
3. What is the percentage of alcoholics in your city?
4. What does alcoholism cost your city annually?
5. What local treatment centers are available?
6. What is the cure rate of AA treatment?
7. Current news reports indicate a high level of alcoholism amoung teenagers in the U.S.. What reasons can you give for this?
8. If your friend were an alcoholic would you make any effort to help him/her? If so, what would you do?

BIOGRAPHY

1. Select a famous person (living or dead) whom you admire. Find the following information:

A. List the major accomplishment(s) of this person.
B. List the major influential factors that helped this person achieve fame.
C. Compare two reference sources on this person's life. What details were left out of one of the sources? Were they important details?
D. Identify weaknesses of this character. How were they overcome?
E. Identify the turning point in this person's life. What caused this person to move from unknown to famous?
F. Design a chronological chart of the major developments in this person's life.

CAPITAL PUNISHMENT

1. How many states allow capital punishment?
2. What is your state's stand on capital punishment?
3. What alternatives are used by states that do not allow capital punishment?
4. What crimes do you feel justify capital punishment?
5. What crimes are considered capital offenses?
6. Set up an evaluation T and consider the pros and cons of capital punishment. Are you for or against? Why?
7. What efforts have been made to rehabilitate hardened criminals? How successful have these efforts been?
8. From time to time the news media tells of the arrest of an escaped criminal who has been living a model life for ten or more years as a productive citizen. Friends can't believe that this person is wanted by the law. Do you think in cases like this that justice would be served if the criminal were allowed to continue his or her freedom?

ERA
WOMEN'S RIGHTS

1. Federal laws mandate that women be paid the same as men for doing similar work. Yet, women's salaries continue to be much lower than those of men even though both perform the same job. Can you find a logical explanation for this?
2. If ERA had passed did this mean that women would be drafted for combat duty? In your opinion should women be subject to the draft? Would there be any exceptions?
3. Watch four of your favorite TV situation comedies. Describe the role of women as portrayed in these shows. Describe the role of men. Does TV perpetuate stereotypes?

RESEARCH CARDS

7-8

FOLK LITERATURE

1. Many old tales are repeated in the literature of a variety of countries. Cinderella is a French tale. However, there are 367 known versions of this tale. How many can you find? From what country is each title?

2. Scholars have determined that the MOTHER GOOSE RHYMES are political satire. Research the origin of some of these verses. To whom are the verses referring?

3. American Indian folktales are filled with symbolism related to nature. Analyze one of these tales. What elements in nature do various characters or objects represent?

4. Study the structure of the basic hero tale. Use the structure in developing a plot outline. Write an original tale.

FUTURE STUDIES

List as many space travel terms as you can. Combine these terms to compose a diamante describing space or space travel.

2. Develop a SOLAR SEARS catalog for the year 2025. What items will be most in demand? Figure the current rate of inflation in determining prices for these items.

3. Watch one science fiction television show. List the various types of technology used in the story. Predict which of these will be in general use by the year 2000.

4. Predict the role of the computer in education. Will the computer replace the schools? the teachers? Give evidence to support your prediction.

RESEARCH CARDS 7-8

FUTURE STUDIES II

1. The population of the United States is growing older. What percentage of the population is currently over the age of 50? What percentage will be over the age of 50 by the year 1995? Predict differences which will be evident in a society of older Americans.

2. Medical science has made rapid advances in the past twenty years and even more rapid advances are predicted for the future. Select one of the topics below. Predict what moral or philosophical debates will take place in the future if the discovery becomes a reality:

   a) Cloning
   b) Test tube babies
   c) Cybernetics (freezing bodies until a cure is found)
   d) Other: A discovery of special interest to you.

GREAT GOOFS!

Read: THE WORLD IS FLAT AND OTHER GREAT MISTAKES
by Lawrence Pringle

1. Select one of the great mistakes described in the book. (Example: Marie Curie died of leukemia)

2. Hypothesize the reason for the mistake. (Example: was the error made due to not knowing the facts? taking a risk? ignoring the facts? misjudgment?)

3. Research the topic and support or deny your initial hypothesis.

4. Research and share with your class other great goofs made throughout history that are not in this book.

RESEARCH CARDS

7-8

LEADERSHIP

1. Research the meaning of leadership. Select four well-known leaders of the past. What qualities did they have in common?
2. Prepare a time line of world leaders beginning with the birth of Queen Victoria and ending with the death of John F. Kennedy. Include the issues and events of importance that took place between those two dates and show which leaders were most powerful.
3. Of the four leaders you chose, list the major contribution of each. Which, in your opinion, made the greatest contribution to society? Be prepared to defend your answer.

   Research the elements of a good speech. What in your opinion, was the greatest speech given in the last 100 years? Why did you select this particular speech over all others?

LYRICS (ROCK)

ANALYZE THE LYRICS OF FOUR FAVORITE ROCK SONGS. ANSWER THESE QUESTIONS.

A. How many words in the lyrics would not be found in the dictionary? What are they?
B. How many words in the lyrics would you guess a person over forty would not understand? Give examples.
C. What words in the lyrics do not mean what they say? List the words and give both meanings.
D. Listen to one hour of rock music on the radio. List the songs played. How many were happy? How many told of sadness and despair? From this limited sample, what conclusions can you draw about rock music?

STOCK MARKET

I. Research the stock market and how it operates

2. "Invest" $5000 in the market. Choose your stocks by researching the companies offering the stock.

3. Buy and sell stocks for six weeks. You can use only the $5000 imaginary loan plus any earnings you may receive. At the end of six weeks were you a winner or a loser?

4. What is meant by a bull market? Bear market? During which market would the most buying take place?

5. Are there any women on the floor of the stock exchange? Why do you suppose this has been traditionally a man's field?

TV SHOWS

I. Listen to the theme songs for your favorite shows. In what way does the theme song reflect the style, theme and/or mood of the show?

2. Design a time line of important events in TV history.

3. Write your original criteria for choosing a popular car. Note TV ads for cars. Which of the criteria listed by you did the commerical stress?

4. Support or deny this statement with evidence. The dress of a TV character reveals the basic personality of that character.

5. What is meant by the PACE of a TV show? Why is pacing important?

6. On an evaluation T list the advantages and disadvantages of having cable TV in every home.

DEVELOP A COMPARISON CHART

Quite often interesting information can be obtained by comparing sources of information. Select one of the topics below for a comparison study. Develop a chart of major points or data which shows clearly how the two sources compare.

1. RESULTS OF A NATIONAL POLL   with   RESULTS OF YOUR POLL ON THE SAME TOPIC

2. MOVIE ADVERTISEMENTS (Types of movie available)   TYPES OF MOVIES PEOPLE IN YOUR COMMUNITY WANT TO SEE

3. AMOUNT OF NEWS APPEARING ABOUT MAJOR CANDIDATES   AMOUNT OF NEWS APPEARING ABOUT MINOR CANDIDATES

4. EDITORIAL ON A SUBJECT FOUND IN ONE NEWSPAPER   EDITORIAL ON SAME SUBJECT FOUND IN A DIFFERENT NEWSPAPER

5. CARS MOST OFTEN ADVERTISED FOR SALE   CARS MOST POPULAR IN YOUR COMMUNITY

6. PRODUCTS MOST OFTEN ADVERTISED   PRODUCTS MOST OFTEN PURCHASED

7. ROLE OF WOMEN IN TV COMMERCIALS (active/passive)   ROLE OF MEN IN TV COMMERCIALS (active/passive)

8. VITAL STATISTICS - CURRENT   VITAL STATISTICS - PAST

9. JOBS MOST OFTEN ADVERTISED IN WANT ADS   ECONOMIC CONDITIONS IN YOUR COMMUNITY

10. NUMBER OF COLLEGES IN YOUR COMMUNITY   % OF COLLEGE BOUND GRADUATES IN YOUR LOCAL HIGH SCHOOL

11. MOST OFTEN READ PART OF THE NEWSPAPER   LEAST OFTEN READ PART OF THE NEWSPAPER

12. LEVEL OF SPENDING FOR MAJOR GOVERNMENT PROGRAMS   HOW MOST PEOPLE WANT THEIR TAX MONIES SPENT

Taking A Poll

One way of gathering information is that of poll-taking This is often done before elections to survey the electorate for candidates.

Interesting data can come from polls.

Predict which make of car is most popular in your neighborhood or town.

_____

Use the form below to survey fifteen homes in your neighborhood to see which makes the families drive.

Family#	#cars	#in family	Makes of Cars
1			
2			
3			
4			
5			
6			
7			
8			
9			
10			
11			
12			
13			
14			
15			

What conclusions can you draw from your poll?
Make a graph or a chart to show your conclusions are valid.

A UNIT ON LEARNING STYLES

A learning styles quiz.

Score your reaction to the following statements on a one to five scale. If you feel the statement is completely true score it a five; if not at all true, score a one; if moderately so, score a three; etc.

1. The best directions to students are told or written. _____
2. Students should keep their feelings to themselves. _____
3. Students to learn well should do one thing at a time. _____
4. Students should be told how to do things. _____
5. Students should have a quiet atmosphere when trying to solve problems. _____
6. Students should be guided in what and how to learn. _____
7. Students like to answer easy questions. _____
8. Students should use the information they read about. _____
9. Students do not have to visualize information in a problem in order to solve it. _____
10. Students learn best when the teacher explains the lesson to them. _____
11. Science is a more important subject than art. _____
12. Simple concepts must be learned before more advanced concepts are taught. _____
13. Learning history is more important than predicting what the world might be like in the future. _____
14. Students should write everything about an answer to a problem before solving it. _____
15. Students learn best in a quiet, orderly classroom. _____

TOTAL _____

Styles

LB = Left brain dominant. Linear, sequential, concrete, accepts authority. Likes correct answers and much structure.

RB = Right brain dominant. Intuitive, perceptive, deals with abstracts, likes confusion, learns from many sources, affective, unstructured, creative.

WBL= Whole brain dominance leaning to the left. Likes structure and linear learning but also likes to deal with the abstract, enjoys the theoretical.

WBR= Whole brain dominance leaning to the right. Likes flexible structure, many different experiences, uses insight, likes logical problem solving, creative in at least one area.

Score

56-75 Left Brain dominant (LB)
37-55 Whole Brain dominant, leaning to the left (WBL)
18-36 Whole Brain dominant, leaning to the right (WBR)
 1-17 Right Brain dominant (RB)

Learning Styles (continued)

I. List as many instructional techniques as you can that teachers use to present information to a class.
    Examine your list. Which techniques would appeal most to RB learners? Which to LB learners?

_____ _____ _____ _____

_____ _____ _____ _____

_____ _____ _____ _____

_____ _____ _____ _____

_____ _____ _____ _____

_____ _____ _____ _____

II. Each learning style has its own characteristic behaviors. After examining these behaviors, identify the learning style of the following literary characters and world leaders.

Literary Characters   World Leaders

EBENEZER SCROOGE _____   GHANDI _____

PETER PAN _____   GOLDA MIER _____

MARY POPPINS _____   ABRAHAM
                                    LINCOLN _____
TOAD (from Wind
       in the   MARGARET
       Willows) _____   THATCHER _____

III. With your group, select four other well known persons (either real or literary). Write their names on the lines below and identify their learning styles.

_____

_____

_____

_____

IV. Cite one major advantage and one disadvantage of being aware of your own dominant learning style.

_____

_____

_____

_____

LEADERSHIP

Comparing Famous Leaders

Leadership can be positive or negative yet great leaders have many things in common. Discover these common traits by completing the chart below.

LEADERS

COMMON FACTORS	Ghandi	Martin Luther King Jr.	Julius Caesar	Hitler	Abe Lincoln	Golda Meir	Mother Theresa	Juan Peron	Joseph Stalin	Napoleon
lost one or both parents at an early age										
wealthy family										
college education										
good speaking ability										
set major goals early in life										
same profession as one or both parents										
used leadership ability positively										
used leadership ability negatively										

Analysis of Data: After analyzing the chart it is evident that gifted leaders--

1. _____

2. _____

SEND A MESSAGE: Write a letter of advice from one of the leaders listed above to another. The letter should reveal what both had in common and the advice should be that which could well have been given if they had both lived at the same time.

KOHLBERG'S STAGES OF MORAL DEVELOPMENT

Stage One: Obey rules to avoid pain or punishment.

Stage Two: Obey rules to obtain rewards or favors.

Stage Three: Follow rules to avoid dislike or disapproval of others.

Stage Four: Obey to avoid punishment by authorities..legal or religious beliefs govern life.

Stage Five: Major concern is the welfare of the nation or community. Rights of all men put before self.

Stage Six: Conform to a self-formulated law (not religious) more important than all laws of men.

The following quotations are taken from David Melton's **Images of Greatness.**
Independence Press   1979

WHERE WOULD YOU RANK THESE PEOPLE IN STAGES OF MORAL
DEVELOPMENT BASED ONLY ON THE QUOTE. SUPPORT OR DENY YOUR
RANKING BY FINDING OUT MORE ABOUT THE LIVES OF THOSE WHO
INTEREST YOU.

_____ 1. "If you refuse to accept anything but the best, you very often get it." W. Somerset Maugham
_____ 2. "Don't put no constrictions on da people. Leave em ta hell alone." Jimmy Durante
_____ 3: "People grow old by deserting their ideals." Albert Einstein
_____ 4. "Everything that is wrong with the world is caused by a lack of moral conviction." Benjamin Spock
_____ 5. "Freedom is life's supreme value and must be preserved at whatever cost." Sam Ervin
_____ 6. "Retire, are you kidding? Fish don't applaud, do they?" Bob Hope
_____ 7. "Duty, honor, country." Douglas MacArthur
_____ 8. "I believe the welfare of each is bound up in the welfare of all." Helen Keller
_____ 9. "Too much of a good thing is wonderful." Mae West
_____ 10. "Do your duty and history will do you justice". Harry Truman

Kohlberg, Lawrence.   Stages of Moral Development.
© 1958 Phi Delta Kappan, 1975 61,10.

CROSSROADS!

Many people have crossroads in their lives when important decisions that are made alter the course of those lives. Below are descriptions of three crossroads:

1. Select one of the decisions to be made.
2. List alternatives on the decision grid.
3. List criteria to consider in choosing one alternative.
4. Score each alternative. Which is best?
5. Research the life of the person to see what decision was actually made. Do the alternatives (yours and his) match?

School or Laboratory?

I. Your name is Thomas Alva Edison. You are an enthusiastic and inventive young man who has managed to make a growing and prosperous business out of selling newspapers, candy, fruit and vegetables while at the same time conducting your own personal laboratory where you perform a variety of experiments - all at the age of fifteen. You have been offered a chance to learn all there is to know about becoming a telegraph operator. Once this has been accomplished your friend (the person offering to teach you) claims that he will do everything in his power to assist you in finding a job.

Should you decide to accept this offer it must mean that you devote eighteen hours a day to the mastery of telegraphy. Your entire income will be shut off and you will be forced to rely on your savings and have no time to work on your own experiments. Should you accept this offer?

Security or the Unknown

II. It is the year 1891 and you, Henry Ford, have just returned from repairing an Otto engine at a soda-bottling company in Detroit, Michigan. You believe that you can adapt this machine for use in a road vehicle which would act as a power-plant for a "horseless carriage," but it is necessary that you learn more about electricity. You have been offered a position in Detroit at the Edison Illuminating Company as an engineer. This experience will undoubtedly give you the experience necessary to carry out your plans.

You currently reside on an 80 acre farm in Dearborn, Michigan where you have your own machine shop and are doing quite well financially for yourself and your dear wife, Clara.

You have explained the situation to Clara, but she is aghast at the thought of having to leave her family and close friends. You both realize that the decision to pick up and move will fling you into an existence never before experienced and your financial status shall not only change, but will most probably be somewhat reduced. Do you take the chance?

Which Method?

III. It is the 18th century and your name is Thomas Hopkins Gallaudet. You have recently been introduced to a man by the name of Dr. Mason Fitch Cogswell whose daughter is deaf. He has requested that you aid him in his attempts to educate her and teach her to communicate. You have decided to go to England to study under the Braidwoods (famous family who developed a method for teaching the deaf to communicate using oralism) and learn their methods and then to go on to France to learn the de l'Epee approach to deaf education (based on manualism).

You inform the Braidwoods of your decision to learn the best of both methods and much to your dismay learn that the Braidwoods object seriously to this proposal as their method of teaching is a family secret.

You now must make a decision. Should you stay in England and study under the Braidwoods to learn their method which you know to be highly successful but be sworn to secrecy or should you forget the Braidwoods and their particular approach and go on to Paris to learn more about the de l'Epee approach?

1 ------------- 10 Low High Alternatives	Criteria	Criteria	Criteria

A. According to the grid, the best alternative is: _____

_____

B. The alternative actually chosen by the famous person was _____

_____

RESEARCHING HISTORICAL DECISIONS

Below are two crucial decisions that had to be made during World War II. Use the decision grid to find the best alternative as YOU see it. Research the actual decision that was made. Do your alternatives agree?

A. A SMALL TOWN IN ENGLAND

Early in World War II British Intelligence cracked the secret German code giving the British advance warning of enemy troop movements, attacks and strengths. One code message was intercepted indicating a bomb attack on a vital town that served as a shipping port in England. Prime Minister Winston Churchill had to decide whether to warn and evacuate the town or refrain from giving the warning so that the enemy would not know its code had been broken. Did he have any alternatives? What would you do?

B. THE BOMB

Several months before the end of World War II, President Harry Truman was informed of the readiness of a devastating bomb that could wipe out an entire city. Some advisors told him to order the dropping of the bomb on major cities in Japan to bring a quick ending to the war. Others said that the victory of the U.S. was already assured and that dropping such a bomb would make the U.S. a monster in the eyes of the rest of the world. Truman had to decide! What factors did he weigh? What other information did he need? What would you decide? Research the decision. Did you agree?

Score: 1=low 5=high or
  1=no
  2=maybe
  3=yes
ALTERNATIVES
	CRITERIA	CRITERIA	CRITERIA

POWER

A Unit to Explore for Middle Grade/Junior High Students.

1. On another sheet of paper list all the names that come to mind when you think of power. (Remember to consider all aspects of society, not just government.)

2. Of the power people you named, in what categories can you group them? (For example, are they in politics, sports, medicine etc.)

3. Many times throughout history a person of high position has been greatly influenced by a person behind the scenes. Can your group name any instances where this has been true?

4. Name three television shows in which the quest for or maintenance of power is the dominant theme. Are there more than three?

5. As a group decide what similar personality traits powerful people possess.

6. Using the Kohlberg scale of moral development choose five powerful individuals (past or present) and compare them on the scale.

Name of Individual	Level One	Level Two	Level Three	Level Four	Level Five	Level Six

7. Go back in time and choose any powerful person of the past. You are his/her historical advisor. If you could give two pieces of advice or information which would have enabled him/her to act more wisely, what would you tell them with your great knowledge of the world since his/her time?

   A. Name:

   Advice

   1.

   2.

8. As editor of a major metropolitan newspaper you have the power to select what news the people will read. The following stories have just come across your desk. You have room on the front page for only one. Rank order them in order of importance:

   CURE FOR CANCER FOUND
   FIRST GASLESS CAR ROLLS OFF ASSEMBLY LINE
   UNEMPLOYMENT DOWN TO 2%
   PLANE CRASH KILLS 350 PEOPLE
   EARTHQUAKE DESTROYS OVER HALF OF BOLIVIA

9. You are the head of a small but profitable corporation. A much larger corporation wishes to buy your company. Your employees have been very loyal to you throughout the years, and while you will basically retain your position, much of your company will be rearranged. What are the pros and cons of agreeing to the sale?

   Pros   Cons

10. At what level of Bloom's Cognitive Taxonomy would you place each of the preceeding nine activities?

150

FIELD INVESTIGATION
The Cemetery

SUGGESTED USE: Grade 6-8
                 Math
                 Language Arts
                 Art
                 Social Studies
                 Science

OBJECTIVE

Use the tools of the social sciences to acquire and communicate information, including maps, charts, graphs, and primary sources.

INSTRUCTIONAL OBJECTIVES:

Affective Objectives: (Attitudes - Values)
1. Identify feelings toward the cemetery.
2. Through direct experience in historical research one can appreciate a state's past.

Cognitive Objectives: (Knowledge-intellectual skills)
1. Accurately collect and graph data from tombstones.
2. Write an epitaph for some famous person from your state.
3. Determine the materials from which tombstones are made.
4. Organize and compile data from the cemetery to consider changes in life span due to several environmental and physical factors.
5. Observe wildlife and plant life associated with cemeteries.

Psychomotor Objectives: (Movement)
1. Make tombstone rubbings
2. Draw maps of the cemetery.

UNDERSTANDING:

A cemetery offers a beginning in the study of life cycles (human, plant, and animal) while starting a study of the local community. Further, this could lead to development of an environmental quality index for the school or neighborhood.

STRATEGY:

Field investigation.

SKILLS:

Classify, research, analyze, collect, graph, draw, map, and discuss.

KEY WORDS:

Epitaph - an inscription in memory of a deceased person.
Wildlife cover - plants, grasses, berries, etc.; food for animals.

MATERIALS/PREPARATION:

Clipboards, pencils, data sheets (sample included), blank newsprint, crayons or charcoal, masking tape, charcoal fixer or hair spray.

FIELD INVESTIGATION

The Cemetery

Have you ever gone to the cemetery for anything other than a funeral? Fear and dread of cemeteries has arisen over the centuries. Many of these fears and social attitudes come from books and movies showing the cemetery as an evil place, full of ghosts and monsters.

How do you feel about taking a field trip to the cemetery? When you think of a cemetery, what kind of feelings come to your mind? The subject of death and burial could be discussed with the class. Make a list of your (or the pupils) feelings and experiences about cemeteries. What is the source of those feelings?

Most cemeteries are beautiful places with trees, flowers, ponds, animals, birds, and interesting tombstones. They are beautiful because of love; love for the persons buried there.

Select a large cemetery that dates from the 1800's to the present. Older cemeteries offer more interesting tombstones for art and language art activities. Get permission to use the cemetery for study.

The class should be divided into small groups and assigned to specific portions of the cemetery. A data sheet should be completed with 20 names from headstones.

ACTIVITIES:

Activity 1.

a. Complete data sheet by making a census of the cemetery.
b. Construct a family tree if the information is available.
c. Map the distribution of graves in the cemetery showing roads, fences, family plots, trees and wildlife cover.

INFORMATION SHEET

THE CEMETERY

Name _____

Group Number _____

Date _____

Name of Deceased	Birth			Death			Age	Male	Female	Family Plot	Veteran	Childbirth	Religion	Type of Marker							
	Day	Month	Year	Day	Month	Year								Granite	Marble	Limestone	Sandstone	Wood	Slab	Block	Post

Names of Family Plots:

Types of Trees found:

During what period did most people die?

19th Century? _____

20th Century? _____

What could be some possible reasons for this difference?

153

Activity 2.

Calculate or graph the following:

a. The number of deaths contrasted with year of death.
b. Compare the average age of death (male, female, infants) before 1900 and after 1900.
c. Determine the number of deaths by month of year.
d. The number of female deaths associated with childbirth.
e. Compare the month of birth with month of death.
f. Average age of death for the cemetery.
g. Number of male and female deaths against age of death (wars, childbirth, epidemic, natural disasters).
h. Graph the death of soldiers per year.
i. In a given period, did men or women die younger?
j. Who is the oldest, youngest?
k. Did more people die in the 1800-1850's, the 1850's to 1900's, the 1900's to the 1950's, or the 1950's to the 1970's?

Activity 3.

a. Review local history for any epidemics or disasters.
b. Compile a list of all occupations discovered from the stones. How have the occupations changed through the years?
c. What evidence of famous people and/or historical events can be seen in the cemetery? Research the lives of famous people buried in the cemetery.

Activity 4.

Epitaphs can be interesting, humorous and very revealing.

a. Collect epitaphs.
b. What does the epitaph tell us about the person, his family and friends or his life?
c. Do the epitaphs tell how the individual died?
d. Write an epitaph for some famous person, such as Mark Twain, President Truman, Eugene Field, Jesse James, or Thomas Hart Benton.

Activity 5.

Headstones are made from many different materials.

a. Count the different types and note the unusual ones.
b. Observe weathering, growth of algae and lichen.
c. Look for the stone carver's name (usually in the lower righthand corner).

Activity 6
   Visit other cemeteries. Compare and contrast the differences in data you gather.

Source: Gordon Griffin, Missouri Department of Conservation.
Reprinted with permission.

154

Putting IT ALL Together!

PRODUCING A LOCAL HISTORY REFERENCE BOOK*

Objective:
In becoming familiar with and using a variety of reference sources, the student will prepare a community reference publication.

Materials/Resources Needed
Twelve reference cards
Access to school and public libraries
Access to community resources
Basic reference works; dictionary, biographical dictionary, atlas, almanac.

Procedure
1. The student should become familiar with basic reference tools which provide the organizational scheme for his or her own local history book.

2. The student proceeds (in any desired order) to work on those sections of the Community Reference Book described on activity cards one through nine.

3. The completion of many of the activity cards will require pre-planning on the part of the student. The following guide will help.

```
Project _____

Materials      _____    _____
Needed
               _____    _____

               _____    _____

Sources of     _____    _____
Information
               _____    _____

Implementation

Step One    _____

Step Two    _____

Step Three  _____
```

*Adapted from CURRICULUM UNITS FOR GIFTED STUDENTS, Missouri Department of Elementary and Secondary Education, 1983. With permission.

I. OVERVIEW

The purpose of this unit is to provide the gifted student with opportunities to use a variety of sources and information effectively. These opportunities include preparation of a community reference publication. This publication should represent a comprehensive compilation of the best research references and community resources available to the student in his particular locale. Interviewing and research skills are emphasized as the student is involved in research which will help him to compile the materials needed for his publication. The publication may take the form of an almanac, atlas, biographical dictionary, or a reference book which combines the three formats. Unit materials include information and planning sheets. It is suggested that the student complete a bibliography of research materials as part of the publication.

II. GOALS

To learn to use a variety of sources and information effectively by:

A. surveying reference books as a research tool.
B. investigating the community as a resource.
C. compiling information from the research materials and resources.
D. using information gathered from research when planning projects.
E. recording and summarizing references and resource materials.

III. INSTRUCTIONAL OBJECTIVES

The student will be able to:

A. show an understanding of research tools. (See Research/Reference Skills Taxonomy in this book)
B. apply information by using a reference book format to communicate information compiled by research.
C. analyze by comparing the ways reference books approach information.
D. plan by organizing time, materials, and resources necessary to complete the project.
E. evaluate by assessing the appropriate resources and information needed.
F. communicate by producing a reference book.
G. think productively by elaborating on a topic in a variety of ways.
H. characterize by evaluating, comparing, and reporting on information obtained from human sources.
I. plan by identifying the project, listing materials needed, following steps for completion, and anticipating and solving problems which may arise.
J. evaluate by assessing his progress and participation in the unit.

IV. TEACHING STRATEGIES

Introduction to the teacher:

A. In order to successfully present this unit, the teacher will need to duplicate the student materials (as explained below).

B. It is suggested that the unit begin with a short introduction by the teacher of the goal for the unit - to plan and produce a community reference publication which follows the format of an alamac, an atlas, a biographical dictionary, or combination of the three formats. The information sheets should then be presented. The student is to choose the research format he will use to complete the publication. He will then be presented with the appropriate planning sheet. The planning sheet will then act as the student/teacher guide for the rest of the unit.

STUDENT MATERIALS

1. Information sheets 1-4

   The purpose of the information sheets is to introduce the child to the various research tool formats. The sheets also contain the student project goal and the requirements of each.

2. Planning sheets 1-4

C. It is suggested that the teacher review or introduce the necessary research skills before beginning the unit activities. See the Taxonomy of Research Skills in this book.

V. REVIEW OF INTERVIEWING STRATEGIES

Whether students interview someone on the telephone or in person, they need to follow certain procedures in order to get the most information from the source.

A. Introduce yourself to the person you want to interview. Explain that you would like an interview and the purpose for the interview.

B. Arrange a time and place for the interview. Choose a place with few distractions.

C. Prepare your questions before the interview. Avoid questions that can be answered with yes or no. Many good questions begin with who, what, where, when or how. Write down your questions.

D. Write down the answers or tape record the interview. If a tape recorder is used, play it during the entire interview. Constantly turning the recorder on and off is distracting to both parties.

An almanac is a book of facts about the world. It is usually published every year and contains up-to-date information on famous people, sports, motion pictures, weather, politics, etc.

Project Goals:
Your almanac should be a book about your community. It should be an up-to-date reference book about people, places, and points of interest and information about your area. Your almanac should contain information about at least ten of the following topics.

1. Agriculture (types of crops, livestock, etc.).

2. Awards, medals, and prizes awarded in your town (including the names of recent recipients).

3. Colleges and universities in your area (including types of degrees and programs offered).

4. Corporations and large businesses (types).

5. Disasters (last five years).

6. Discoveries and inventions.

7. Economics (trends).

8. Educational statistics (current and expected trends).

9. Elections (results of most recent elections).

10. Famous people.

11. Flags (of municipalities, organizations, clubs, etc.).

12. Landmarks.

13. Laws and documents (of special interest to young people).

14. Memorable dates in town's history.

15. Meteorological data (climate and weather information).

16. Parks (national, state, county, local and locations).

17. Population information.

18. Sports (professional, amateur, school associated).

19. Surveys of resident preferences - T.V. shows, movies, books, cars, pets.

20. Any other topic of interest.

PLANNING SHEET 1 - ALMANAC PLANNING SHEET

NAME _____ DATE _____

A. PROJECT: Almanac based on information about and for my community.

B. TOPICS: (List under Column 1)

C. REFERENCES AND RESOURCES TO CONTACT: (List under Column 2)

COLUMN 1   COLUMN 2

1. _____   1. _____

2. _____   2. _____

3. _____   3. _____

4. _____   4. _____

5. _____   5. _____

D. MATERIALS NEEDED:

_____   _____

_____   _____

_____   _____

_____   _____

E. FORMAT: Index, charts, graphs, pictures, tables, articles, bibliography,
             etc.

F. IMPLEMENTATION: (Steps to take to complete project)

Step One _____

Step Two _____

Step Three _____

Step Four _____

G. PROBLEMS/SOLUTIONS: (Problems I may encounter and Solutions   to
                          those problems)

_____

_____

_____

_____

INFORMATION SHEET 2 - THE ATLAS

An atlas is a book of maps, graphs, and tables giving geographic information. These may include physical, political, and other types of maps.

Project Goal:
Your atlas should be a book of geographic information about your community. It should also contain maps, graphs, and tables. Your atlas should contain information about at least ten of the following topics.

1. Aerial views.

2. Crops.

3. Wildlife.

4. Weather/climate.

5. Parks and camp sites.

6. Physical maps (rivers, mountains, etc.).

7. Political maps (county, city boundaries).

8. Highways.

9. Places of interest.

10. Airplane routes.

11. Railroad lines.

12. Population centers.

13. Early historical information (ex. Indian tribes).

14. Political divisions (townships, precincts, etc.).

15. Any topic of interest.

PLANNING SHEET 2 - ATLAS PLANNING SHEET

NAME _____ DATE _____

A. PROJECT: Atlas based on geographic information of your community.

B. TOPICS: (List under Column 1)

C. REFERENCES AND RESOURCES TO CONTACT: (List under Column 2)

COLUMN 1   COLUMN 2

   1. _____   1. _____

   2. _____   2. _____

   3. _____   3. _____

   4. _____   4. _____

   5. _____   5. _____

D. MATERIALS NEEDED:

   _____   _____

   _____   _____

   _____   _____

   _____   _____

E. FORMAT: Index, charts, graphs, pictures, tables, articles, bibliography,
            etc.

F. IMPLEMENTATION: (Steps to take to complete project)

Step One _____

Step Two _____

Step Three _____

Step Four _____

G. PROBLEMS/SOLUTIONS: (Problems I may encounter and Solutions   to
                          those problems)

_____

_____

_____

_____

INFORMATION SHEET 3 - THE BIOGRAPHICAL DICTIONARY

A biographical dictionary contains short biographies of famous people. The biographies can be about persons living or dead.

Project Goals:
Your biographical dictionary should contain short biographies about people from your community. They can be famous or important persons who are living or dead. Your biographical dictionary should contain information about at least fifteen of the following people.

1. Mayor or other elected official.

2. Top political party leader.

3. Professional or amateur athlete or coach.

4. School board member.

5. Educator.

6. Law enforcement official.

7. Medical professional.

8. Civic-minded organizational leader (ex. president-Jaycees).

9. Business leader.

10. Transportation official.

11. Entertainment personality.

12. Conservation leader.

13. Newspaper editor or reporter.

14. Religious leader.

15. Founding father or early settler.

16. Artist or musician.

17. Actor, actress or theatrical director.

18. Author.

19. Agricultural leader.

20. War hero.

21. T.V. broadcaster.

22. Union leader.

23. Legendary or famous person of the past.

24. Scientist.

25. Leading merchant.

26. Anyone else of interest.

PLANNING SHEET 3 - BIOGRAPHICAL DICTIONARY PLANNING SHEET

NAME _____ DATE _____

A. PROJECT: Biographical dictionary about people from your community.

B. TOPICS: (List under Column 1)

C. REFERENCES AND RESOURCES TO CONTACT: (List under Column 2)

COLUMN 1   COLUMN 2

1. _____   1. _____

2. _____   2. _____

3. _____   3. _____

4. _____   4. _____

5. _____   5. _____

D. MATERIALS NEEDED:

_____   _____

_____   _____

_____   _____

_____   _____

E. FORMAT: Index, charts, graphs, pictures, tables, articles, bibliography,
           etc.

F. IMPLEMENTATION: (Steps to take to complete project)

Step One _____

Step Two _____

Step Three _____

Step Four _____

G. PROBLEMS/SOLUTIONS: (Problems I may encounter and Solutions to
                        those problems)

_____

_____

_____

_____

INFORMATION SHEET 4 - REFERENCE BOOK

A reference book contains a variety of information in a variety of ways. Current facts, maps, charts, graphs, and biographical information may be included.

Project Goals:
Your reference book should be a combination almanac, atlas, and biographical dictionary (see information sheets 1, 2, and 3). Your reference book should include a total of ten topics combined from the three information sheets. As before, your reference book should be based on the community.

PLANNING SHEET 4 - REFERENCE BOOK PLANNING SHEET

NAME _____ DATE _____

A. PROJECT: Reference book based on information for and about your community.

B. TOPICS: (List under Column 1)

C. REFERENCES AND RESOURCES TO CONTACT: (List under Column 2)

COLUMN 1   COLUMN 2

1. _____   1. _____

2. _____   2. _____

3. _____   3. _____

4. _____   4. _____

5. _____   5. _____

6. _____   6. _____

7. _____   7. _____

8. _____   8. _____

9. _____   9. _____

10. _____   10. _____

D. MATERIALS NEEDED:

_____   _____

_____   _____

_____   _____

_____   _____

PLANNING SHEET 4 - REFERENCE BOOK PLANNING SHEET

E. FORMAT: (Combined format - see Planning Sheets 1, 2, and 3)

F. IMPLEMENTATION: (Steps to take to complete project)

Step One: _____

_____

Step Two: _____

_____

Step Three: _____

_____

Step Four: _____

_____

G. PROBLEMS/SOLUTIONS: (Problems which I may encounter and possible
solutions to those problems.)

_____

_____

_____

_____

_____

_____

_____

_____

_____

PRODUCING A LOCAL HISTORY REFERENCE BOOK

ACTIVITY 1

THE ENCYCLOPEDIA

Begin your reference book with encyclopedia entries. Include information on Agriculture - Businesses - Colleges - Discoveries - Economic Trends - Famous People - Landmarks - Government - Climate - Parks - Sports - Recreation.

ACTIVITY 2

DICTIONARY

Prepare a dictionary of words and expressions with definitions of local words and phrases used and understood by most people in your community but not used as often or in the same way in other parts of the country.

ACTIVITY 3

ATLAS

The atlas section of your book can contain at least six of the following:
Physical map of your city
Political map of your city
Crop, wildlife or weather maps
Highways, airline and/or rail routes
Places of interest.

ACTIVITY 4

THE LIBRARY

Visit your public library. Ask about available materials on local history. Take notes on interesting people and events in your city's past to be included in your reference book.

ACTIVITY 5

DEWEY DECIMAL SYSTEM

Conclude your reference book with a Dewey Decimal System story about an interesting historical event concerning your city.
Follow a pattern similar to those given on pages 42 and 43 .

ACTIVITY 6

CARD CATALOG

Prepare a series of subject cards (following the correct form) for major topics covered in your book. Obtain blank cards from your school librarian.

RESEARCH   CARD 7

An almanac is a book of facts about the world. It is usually published every year and contains up-to-date information about famous people, sports, motion pictures, weather, politics, etc.

Include an almanac section in your book.

ACTIVITY 7

ALMANAC

Include up-to-date information on the following:

Awards
Disasters
Educational Statistics
Elections
Flags
Unusual laws
Memorable dates
Population information

RESEARCH   CARD 8

BIOGRAPHICAL DICTIONARY

Provides basic information in short entry form on prominent people. Entries appear alphabetically by last name.

Personal interviews may be needed with famous persons you want to include or with those who knew them in your community.

ACTIVITY 8

BIOGRAPHICAL DICTIONARY

Your biographical dictionary section should include short biographies of well-known people in your community.

Ideas for Research

Mayor	Newspaper editor
Professional athlete or coach	Religious leader
Educator	Early settler
Law official	Artist
Doctor	Musician
Club leader	Actor/Actress
Business leader	Author
Entertainer	TV or radio person

RESEARCH   CARD 9

THE COMMUNITY AS A RESOURCE

Your town or city is a valuable resource in finding out more about a subject. Use the telephone directory to find experts in the area of interest to you. Good telephone manners and prepared interview questions will usually bring you excellent results.

Check READER'S GUIDE for those articles that have appeared about your community in magazines!

ACTIVITY 9

COMMUNITY AS A RESOURCE

Prepare and report on surveys of resident preferences in your community.

Possible Topics

TV Shows	Cars
Books	Pets
Foods	Political affiliation

EVALUATION

This form should be completed by the student. A similar form is to be completed by the teacher. Forms are compared and differences reconciled through a student-teacher conference.

	Low									High
1. Understanding and use of basic reference tools	1	2	3	4	5	6	7	8	9	10
2. Use of extensive resources	1	2	3	4	5	6	7	8	9	10
3. Effective interview techniques	1	2	3	4	5	6	7	8	9	10
4. Organization of data in reference book format	1	2	3	4	5	6	7	8	9	10
5. Effective use of time	1	2	3	4	5	6	7	8	9	10
6. Careful planning of steps, materials, resources used in project	1	2	3	4	5	6	7	8	9	10
7. Inclusion of unusual and interesting information	1	2	3	4	5	6	7	8	9	10
8. Use of higher level questions for research	1	2	3	4	5	6	7	8	9	10
9. Selection for inclusion of important and interesting information (VS unimportant, uninteresting)	1	2	3	4	5	6	7	8	9	10
10. Final product has attractive format	1	2	3	4	5	6	7	8	9	10
11. Careful editing for errors	1	2	3	4	5	6	7	8	9	10
12. Use of effective illustrations	1	2	3	4	5	6	7	8	9	10
13. Gained greater understanding of my community, its history and people	1	2	3	4	5	6	7	8	9	10
14. Good use of summarizing and recording skills	1	2	3	4	5	6	7	8	9	10
15. Other criteria	1	2	3	4	5	6	7	8	9	10

Total Score _____ (Possible 150)

NAME _____

TAG A TALENT TEST ONE p. 24
Productive Thinking 2,9,3,13
Forecasting 4
Decision Making 6,11,7,14
Planning 8,12,16
Communication 1,5,15,18,10,17

TAG A TALENT TEST TWO p 25
Productive Thinking 1,11,15,6
Forecasting 3
Decision Making 9,7,13,2
Planning 5,17,12
Communication 18,4,8,16,10,14

INCOGNITO TITLES p. 35
1. Born Free
2. Call of the Wild
3. Curious George Goes to the Hospital
4. Frosty the Snowman
5. Green Eggs and Ham
6. Little Engine that Could
7. Puss in Boots
8. Steadfast Tin Soldier
9. Stolen Fire
10. Wit and Wisdom of Fat Albert

TRACK DOWN p. 36
astrology, zodiac, capricornus, goat, wool, Andes, Himalaya, snow, six, chambers.
Whittaker Chambers

REFERENCE MATH p. 37
1) 5 2) 10,50 3) 6, 300
4) 3, 100 5) 5, 20 6) 23, 460 7) 2, 462 8) 6, 77
9) 23, 100 10) 2, 50

SCARY BOOKS p. 40

Across	Down
1. Coombs	1. Corbett
2. Adams	2. Konigsburg
3. Norton	3. Benchley
4. Estes	4. Snyder
5. Singer	5. Flieshman
6. Bright	6 Leach
7. Bennett	

BEST OF SCIENCE FICTION p. 41

Across	Down
1. Mushroom	1. Runaway
2. Enchantress	2. Wrinkle
3. Ka'at	3. Eyes
4. Homework	4. Pickerell
5. Frisby	5. Thousand
6. Solution	6. Space

BAFFLING BATTLES p. 42

weapons	355.8
horses	636.1
railroads	385
ships	387.2
Navy	359.3
Airplanes	629.13
French	914.4
Indians	970.1
Revolutionary War	973.3
England	914.2
the Civil War	973.7
Kentucky	917.69
slavery	326
World War I	940.3
Germany	914.3
Austria	914.36
Hungary	914.39
Bulgaria	914.977
Turkey	915.61
Great Britian	914.2
France	914.4
Russia	914.7
Italy	914.5
Belgium	914.93
United States	917.3
Germany	914.3
Poland	914.38
World War II	940.54
Japan	915.2
United Nations	341.23
time	529

MYTHOLOGY MYSTERY   p. 43

Mythology	292
Greece	938
Rome	937
weather	551.5
seasons	525
stars	523.8
planets	523.4
houses	728
flying	629.1
birds	598.2
sun	523.7
plants	581
food	641.3
music	780
snake	598.1
horses	636.1
dog	636.7

QUICK REFERENCE HANDBOOKS p 47

1. Guinness
2. Kane
3. Brewer
4. Brewer
5. Bartlett
6. Bartlett
7. Guinness
8. Brewer
9. Kane

ALMANAC PRACTICE   p. 49

1. Thomas A Edison
2. since 1927
3. Colorado Springs, CO.
4. William Henry Pratt
5. Bela Lugosi Blasko
6. Hungary
7. no
8. Fredric March
9. Wallace Berry in THE CHAMP
   Fredric March in DR. JEKYLL
   AND MR HYDE

REFERENCE SOURCE QUICKCHECK   p.51

1. Almanac
2. Biographical Dict./Encyclopedia
3. Dictionary of Synonyms
4. Biographical Dict./Encyclopedia
5. Atlas
6. Almanac
7. Encyclopedia
8. Atlas
9. Reader's Guide
10. Dictionary of Synonyms
11. Encyclopedia
12. Atlas
13. Dictionary
14. Almanac

PHOTO PUZZLERS: ONE   p. 128

No Fishing sign a joke. This
bridge spans the Royal Gorge
in Colorado. River lies thousands
of feet below.
Statue: made of car bumpers
Yucca Plant: baskets, needles,
ropes, mats, clothing, roofing
sandals, food, soap, medicine.

PHOTO PUZZLERS: TWO p. 129

A) Albert S. Johnston. Battle of
   Shiloh April 6-7, 1862
B) Blue, caused by the density of
   the ice which absorbs all colors
   except blue.

CROSSROADS   p. 146

1. Edison accepted the offer
2. Ford accepted the offer
3. Gallaudet went to Paris

RESEARCHING HISTORICAL DECISIONS   p.148

A. No warning was given to the
   village. It was severely bombed.
B. The bomb was dropped.